Tools of Control or Seeds of Liberation?

Tools of Control or Seeds of Liberation?

Reformed Evangelism and Slavery in the Ante-Bellum American South

Iain Whyte

The Lutterworth Press

THE LUTTERWORTH PRESS

P.O. Box 60
Cambridge
CB1 2NT
United Kingdom

www.lutterworth.com
publishing@lutterworth.com

Paperback ISBN: 978 0 7188 9796 3
PDF ISBN: 978 0 7188 9798 7
ePub ISBN: 978 0 7188 9797 0

British Library Cataloguing in Publication Data
A record is available from the British Library

First published by The Lutterworth Press, 2025

Copyright © Iain Whyte, 2025

All rights reserved. No part of this edition may be reproduced, stored electronically or in any retrieval system, or transmitted in any form or by any means, electronic, mechanical, photocopying, recording, or otherwise, without prior written permission from the Publisher (permissions@lutterworth.com).

Contents

Acknowledgements	vi
Introduction	1
1. John Knox and the Legacy of Religious Education	6
2. New World Presbyterians – Slavery and Caution	13
3. The Dilemmas of Some Princetonians	27
4. Rebellion and Reaction	39
5. Paternalism and Colonialism	53
6. Religious Education and Slaveholding	67
7. Religion in the Memory of the Enslaved	82
8. Against the Odds — Two Self-Liberated Women in a Male Era	96
9. Black Presbyterians in Cooperation and Conflict	110
10. Visiting the Reformation Roots	124
11. In the End of the Day	139
Index	146

Acknowledgements

There are a number of individuals and organisations to whom I am indebted for assistance in the research for and writing of this book. As indicated in the book, the idea came from a conversation during a short visit to the College of Charleston, South Carolina with the now Emeritus Professor Bernard Powers. The late Professor Lawrence Jones taught me in 1966/7 during a Masters course in Union Seminary in New York on 'Negro History' and encouraged my interest in this field. His recent history of African American Churches has been invaluable. Especially valuable have been the scholarly accounts of Southern Presbyterianism by Professor Emeritus Erskine Clarke, formerly of Columbia Seminary, and a friend for many years.

I have been assisted in the research for this book by many libraries in many places – Columbia Seminary in Georgia, The College of Charleston (especially from its former Archivist Dr Harlan Greene), The Avery Institute in Charleston, Boston Public Library, The Mitchell Library, Glasgow. Gladstone's Residential Library in Hawarden, Wales, has been a haven for me and may scholars on a number of occasions. But I have spent the most time in the peaceful Reading Room of the National Library of Scotland in Edinburgh. The kind helpfulness and friendly atmosphere amongst the staff towards readers in the NLS makes it a superb venue.

I wish to acknowledge financial assistance in enabling me to undertake research visits from the The Carnegie Trust for the Universities of Scotland and the Strathmartine Trust in St Andrews, and for publication from the Drummond Trust in Stirling. James Clarke have been an excellent publisher to work with and Sarah Algar–Hughes the Co-editor has patiently coped with my non-technical skills in presentation of the manuscript.

The encouragement of friends on this venture has been so appreciated, not least the African American writer, distinguished musician, pastor and my friend Jimi Calhoun who has kindly contributed a note for the cover.

Finally I wish to dedicate this book to the memory of two people. My late wife Isabel (1943-2002) who for more than 55 years has been amongst so much else a companion in the cause of human rights and a better vision of the world, and someone that I would have loved her to meet, Albert Peters (1869-1965) a friend for two of the most significant weeks in my life.

Note on Terminology

I have tried to be as sensitive as possible in the use of terminology. When I was involved in Civil Rights in the Southern States in 1964 the accepted term in the Movement was 'negro.' I have used the later description 'African American' throughout with a few exception when 'black' seemed appropriate. The hated and despicable 'n....er' word has only been used as a direct quote from slavers or racist speeches or from formerly enslaved people referring to themselves.

From the African American Institute in Boston I learned much about the language that gives dignity and respect. Although 'slave' is occasionally used and 'slavery' is used to denote the system, I have tried to refer to people as 'enslaved', thus putting the emphasis on the treatment rather than the identity. In the same way the term 'self-liberated' has been used, testifying to deliberate action by people to gain their freedoms, rather than the tags 'runaway', 'fugitive' or others used by those who held them captive. For the latter I have used inverted commas so as not to give legitimacy to their right to own humans as property. If that appears in the text as slightly awkward, so be it. I felt that it was more important to acknowledge our common humanity than keep to strict semantics.

I have deliberately included the names of all formerly enslaved men and women whose testimony forms Chapter 7, but not extended the index to include the passing references to those who held them captive.

Iain Whyte
January 2025

Introduction

Vladimir Lenin once was reputed to say 'War is a terrible thing. It is also a terribly profitable thing.' The same epithet could apply to the institution of chattel slavery which for several hundred years helped to enrich and develop an expanding world, and where human beings in Africa were transported in their millions to North and South America and condemned to a fate for them and their descendants, when other human beings, mainly of European descent, held absolute power over every aspect of their lives and deaths, with no prospect of an ending.

This has rightly been recognised as one of the greatest of crimes against humanity in human history, and one which lasted for hundreds of years. The twentieth century has been judged to be one that has hardly been surpassed in the sickening disregard for human life and in providing regimes that at times plumbed the depths in human cruelty. Slavery, it is true, could provide examples of humane and caring 'owners', but to read the accounts of the almost unimaginable cruelties, tortures and terrors visited on millions of enslaved peoples, is to realise that modern dictators have invented very few techniques in denying humanity to other human beings.

Although the trade in and transportation of enslaved people was not exclusive to one religion, overwhelmingly chattel slavery was an institution controlled by those who claimed to practise Christianity, and whose countries of origin were part of Christendom. Many of those who went to what became known as the New World had travelled there to shake off the shackles of religious or political persecution. They embraced the concept, as stated in the eighteenth century in the constitution of the most significant of new nations, that 'all men are created equal and have the right to life, liberty, and the pursuit of happiness'.[1]

The question of the incompatibility of slavery and a faith founded in the person of Jesus of Nazareth, was only raised, to any great extent, when the movement for the abolition of the slave trade and slavery itself began in the mid-eighteenth century. Many historians have been unwilling to recognise that the work to have this practice banned by law was led in the main by groups of Christians, in which the Society of Friends (Quakers) played a role well beyond their numbers. It was a mixed picture in England, Scotland and the United States, since many churches were often driven by protection of self-interest rather than humanity. Overall, without the contributions of individuals and groups of people of faith, slavery would in the end have ended, but the human agony that it produced would have been more protracted.

'Was the offer of Christianity and religious education to those who were enslaved in America a tool for control of those enslaved, or was it a means of liberation?' This was a question posed by me some years ago, to the African American historian Professor Bernard Powers in his study in Charleston, South Carolina. He thought for a few moments. 'Overall,' he said, 'it was the latter.'[2] That question is the subject of this book and in answering it the histories of many famous and unknown participants in the ante-bellum period are explored, both black and white. Because religious education was a passion and priority for the Reformers in Europe in the sixteenth century, and especially for those in the Calvinist tradition, many of whose descendants were Scottish and Northern Irish emigrants to the Americas, that tradition is an obvious focus for examining that question.

The starting point is the contribution of John Calvin's most renowned disciple, the fiery Scottish reformer, John Knox, who more than any other helped to lay the foundation of universal education and take seriously the pastoral and evangelical responsibility for the people of the nation, a work which became vital in what emerged as the national Church of Scotland. Calvinism was a curious blend of strict doctrinal control and civic organisation alongside the encouragement of personal faith, evangelism, and opportunity to learn and improve by knowledge. A key factor was the vision of universal literacy, closely

---

1. United States of America, Declaration of Independence, 4 July 1776.
2. Conversation with the author, College of Charleston, 11 Apr 2013.

tied in with the ability to read the scriptures, something which, the Reformers claimed, had been denied by the Roman Catholic Church in Scotland.

The book examines the pre- and post-independence United States of America, and the attitudes of those churches from the Reformed and Presbyterian tradition towards enslaved people. The early public records within the Presbyterian Church in America reflect the dilemmas that churchmen faced, between condemnation of what one historian described as 'The Peculiar Institution',[3] and the need to hold onto the support of their members, North and South, thus staving off the split in Presbyterianism which became more inevitable. Church pronouncements were so often hedged about by ambivalence and the watering down of absolutes, and Presbyterians in America, although not alone amongst the Protestant denominations, were conspicuous by their vacillation.

This dilemma was reflected by some of those associated with the early years of that celebrated Presbyterian foundation, Princeton. One of its first Presidents, a minister from Scotland and a signatory to the Declaration of Independence in 1776, never resolved this dilemma in his personal or public life. No more did some of his distinguished contemporaries or students.

One way in which the South sought to find a solution to the irony of slavery in a free society was the embrace of what became known as 'paternalism', a perceived divine trust of care and responsibility for those whose lives were 'entrusted' to them in the natural order of things. It was of course undergirded by the assumption that at worst enslaved men and women were of no better human value than animals, and that at best their humanity was naturally inferior, and that this inferiority was marked entirely by racial characteristics. Paternalism suffered a severe blow in the early and mid-nineteenth century when real or supposed slave rebellions led to fears that the only security for the holders of enslaved people was not kindness, but further harsh repression.

Yet there was always a nagging doubt within the minds of many thinking white people that this whole construction of slavery might be faulty, and even worse, that it could have incurred divine disapproval rather than support. There was another attempt by concerned whites,

---

3. Kenneth Stampp, *The Peculiar Institution: Slavery in the Ante-Bellum South* (New York: Random House, 1956).

undergirded quietly by those who saw it as a racist solution – that of encouraging black Americans, including, but not limited to, enslaved people, to return to their origins by returning to Africa and thus assist a solution to the problem.

African colonisation had in it a strong element of Christian evangelism towards what was seen as a dark and 'heathen' continent receptive and ripe for mission. The nineteenth-century drive for mission overseas was sometimes coupled with the racist conviction that this was a way of diminishing the increasing number of black people in America. It also divided the movement for the abolition of slavery, with many whites believing that it would be a way to weaken slavery and assist its eventual abolition. Some African American leaders for a time embraced this as a way of freeing themselves from America by making a completely new life in the Africa of their ancestors. This was a movement with some that lasted beyond slavery and well into the twentieth century.

The limitations of benevolent evangelism within the structure of slavery is examined through the lives of three major white church figures in Charleston, all influenced by the Reformed tradition of enthusiasm for the religious instruction of enslaved men and women. A vital part of exploring this question is to hear the voices of those who had experienced the life-denying condition of enslavement, and how they perceived and practised the Christian faith within this nightmare. Formerly enslaved elderly men and women in the 1930s were enabled through a public project funded by the US government in the Depression years to reflect on their experiences. Many spoke about attempts to introduce religious education on the plantations, about the ways in which the Bible was employed, and about religious worship controlled or permitted. Much of their testimony is not only unique, but until comparatively recently has remained buried in academic archives, while the reality of American slavery was glossed over by historians, with some distinguished exceptions.

The lives of distinguished women who liberated themselves from slavery are now becoming documented, rather than patronisingly romanticised, in contemporary studies. Their testimonies and their contributions to the anti-slavery movement, have often been subsumed in favour of male abolition leaders. At an early stage the American abolitionist cause was divided on whether to welcome the contribution of white women, and black female activists often had to struggle doubly for acceptance. Yet their faith and its outworking remains a powerful part of the wider picture.

Some black male ministers from the Presbyterian tradition, all of whom rated education as a key to liberation, provided leadership for the abolition movement, but not without controversy or conflict over such key questions as colonisation and evangelism, revolution or cooperation within the system, support for the constitution, or distancing from the Union side in the Civil War.

In the mid-nineteenth century many leading black abolitionists visited and informed British and Irish audiences on the reality of slavery. Some came to avoid recapture, others to rally support. Those who came to Scotland played a strong role in raising awareness amongst ordinary people even during the Civil War, where many ordinary people had sympathy and even supported practical help for the cause of the South, all too easily portrayed as the wronged 'underdog'.

I am more than conscious that as a white Scot who has never known the dehumanising pain of racism, still less the agonies of the 'unfree', I am ill qualified to judge, perhaps even to comment on, the experiences of those whose lives have been so blighted in this way. I can only reflect their words and the documents in which they own and celebrate their courageous struggle.

In my study I have a photograph taken of an elderly gentleman outside his small house in Greenville, Mississippi. I stayed with Mr Albert Peters for some days in 1964 when as a visiting student, I was involved briefly with the Civil Rights Campaign in Mississippi. Mr Peters had been born just four years after slavery was abolished, and he told me tales of his father's experiences. I asked him if he wasn't afraid of the all too frequent attacks or firebombs on houses that hosted student volunteers. 'Lawd no' he said laughing, 'I'm ninety five. I'm going to die soon and go to heaven. What can they do to me now?' Mr Peters was a man of great dignity (leavened by some lovely humour and hospitality) who had lived his life through almost a whole century in the face of the most horrific denial of human rights. He was never a 'victim', because he met all these obstacles with courage, faith and hope, in a battle that is far from won today. To his sacred memory this book is respectfully dedicated.

Chapter 1

John Knox and the Legacy of Religious Education

For the preservation of religion it is most expedient that scholes be universally erected in all cities and chief townes, the oversight whereof to be committed to the magistrates and godly learned men of the said cities and towns.
—John Knox, First Book of Discipline (1560)

John Knox (1514-1572): A Complex Character in a Complex Land

There is a popular characterisation in modern times of Scotland as a land, after achieving its own religious reformation in the mid-sixteenth century, in which its people were subjected to a cold and ruthless religious domination, brought from John Calvin's Geneva, which imposed a new theological slavery upon them. Some, like the late celebrated modern literary figure Tom Nairn, affirmed most of his life that Scotland would not be free until the last Church of Scotland (Presbyterian) minister was strangled by a copy of the *Sunday Post*, a popular and somewhat moralistic newspaper.

Calvinism undoubtedly had a severe and joyless aspect to it which in small quantities has lasted until modern times. A story is told in the mid-eighteenth century of two elders of the Kirk[1] who, faced

---

1. In Scotland the National Church is known colloquially as 'The Kirk'.

with an icy journey to attend worship on the Sabbath day, decided to skate there. Such seeming frivolity led to the two being paraded before their fellow elders and being asked to explain their behaviour and such desecration of the holiness of the Lord's Day. They admitted to the deed, but were exonerated when they solemnly declared that neither of them had derived any pleasure from the experience.

Undoubtedly the most influential religious figure in the second half of the sixteenth century in Scotland was a close friend and disciple of John Calvin of Geneva, John Knox. Knox was born in c.1514 in the town of Haddington, East Lothian. His father is most likely to have been a tenant farmer of the Earl of Bothwell, and John acknowledged the military service that several generations of Knox's had given in the conflict between Scotland and England, culminating for the time in the Battle of Flodden, months before he was born. Being raised in difficult times, with Haddington very much in the front line of further threats of invasion from the South, the young Knox, not having the privilege of being the oldest son in the family and inheriting land, followed that other current avenue for employment – a career in the church. He flourished at the 'Song School' attached to St Mary's Church in Haddington, and his aptitude in studies of liturgy and the Vulgate Bible propelled him towards the priesthood. He attended the University of St Andrews and was ordained a Roman Catholic priest in 1536.[2]

The Scotland within which Knox grew up was reckoned by many to be one of the most culturally backward nations in Western Europe. Certainly it contained in Glasgow, St Andrews and Aberdeen three of the five universities in what would shortly be the United Kingdoms of Scotland and England (the other two being Oxford and Cambridge). Yet the teaching of those who were able to attend these institutions was heavy prescribed and controlled by the Roman Catholic Church. What was different in Scotland was that, whereas Oxford and Cambridge selected their students on the basis of wealth or influence, Scottish universities from the start were places in which gifted young men could find a place, regardless of their ordinary birth.

Under the influence of Patrick Hamilton (1504-28) and George Wishart (1513-46), two early reformers who were later to pay for their allegiance with their lives, Knox became more disillusioned with the

---

2. Jane Dawson, *John Knox* (New Haven: Yale University Press, 2015) pp. 2-4. Professor Dawson's study of the Scottish Reformer has quickly been recognised as the definitive modern one.

Catholic Church. He produced fiery sermons, including one in St Andrews that compared the Pope to the Antichrist. After the murder of Cardinal Beaton in revenge for his execution of Wishart at the stake, the rebels protected Knox. However fortunes changed, and by 1547 St Andrews castle was besieged by the French on the invitation of Mary of Guise. For the next nineteen months John Knox, and other prisoners captured there, were condemned to serve as galley slaves on French ships.[3]

The Reformation in Europe

England had become officially Protestant under the regency of the boy king Edward VI, and on his release, Knox found employment as a priest of the Church of England. It was not a comfortable position, and in sermons in the court and country he sailed close to the wind by attempting to reform the Anglican Prayer Book, and outlawing the practice of kneeling at prayers. In 1554, with the accession of Mary Tudor and England's return to Roman Catholicism, John Knox sailed over the English channel to the continent of Europe.

His first significant encounter with Protestantism in Europe was a meeting with John Calvin in Geneva where, through the latter's influence, he was later to serve as minister of one of the new churches in the city. More immediately, he received an invitation to lead a congregation of English exiles in Frankfurt, something that Calvin encouraged. He found their adherence to the Book of Common Prayer not to his liking, and after he had published a pamphlet attacking the Holy Roman Emperor, in whose domain Frankfurt lay, he had to leave Germany and spent two years preaching and teaching in Geneva.

A brief return to Scotland was made in 1555 at the request of his wife Margery Bowes, who had not followed him into exile. Political power had shifted to Scottish nobles such as the Earls of Moray and Mar, both sympathetic to the Protestant cause, and Knox spent a great deal of time preaching and speaking about Calvinist doctrine. Despite attempts by the bishops to bring him to trial in Edinburgh, there was no action taken by the Queen Regent, to whom he sent a

---

3. This was a familiar fate for defeated enemies of little social status. Its harsh and unremitting conditions led to a very short lifespan as the same did for enslaved people on the plantations in the West Indies.

polite letter which she treated as a joke. It called on her to support the Reformation and dismiss all the bishops.[4]

Knox's time in Geneva prepared him for the kind of role he proposed to play in a Scotland riven with the rivalries of religious parties and the insecure position of Mary of Guise. In January 1559 he left Geneva, but took longer than usual to reach Scotland due to Queen Elizabeth of England's refusal, not for the first time, to issue him a passport to travel through England. Although he was an outlaw by the decree of the Queen Regent, he was well protected by growing Scottish support, and preached in St Andrews and St Giles Cathedral in Edinburgh. Mary of Guise called French and English troops to her aid, but after her death in June 1560 a peace treaty was signed in Edinburgh, foreign troops were sent away and the Protestants were firmly in the saddle of power.

Forging A New 'Godly Commonwealth'

Within days Parliament adopted the Scots Confession of Faith, condemned doctrine and practice contrary to the Reformed faith, revoked the jurisdiction in Scotland of the Pope and forbad celebration of the Mass.[5] At Knox's moment of triumph his wife died, leaving him to care for two young children. This in no way cooled his zeal in challenging the young Mary Queen of Scots. On an early encounter, when she asked him whether subjects had a right to resist a ruler, he responded that if they exceeded their lawful limits, they might be resisted. Yet he qualified this by differentiating between active and passive resistance, and contended that madness or persecution in the behaviour of rulers justified rebellion. Some of the Protestant nobles, fearing that Knox's extremism might force a total breakdown of relationships between the Kirk and the Queen, cited Calvin as a source of the duty of obedience to the authorities. Knox for his part was disappointed not to get a response from his mentor in Geneva

---

4. G. MacGregor, *The Thundering Scot* (Philadelphia: Westminster Press, 1957), pp. 81-83.
5. The Scots Confession of Faith 1560. This document and the First Book of Discipline were drawn up by a group of six ministers, all of whom happened to have John as their Christian names! Although Knox played a crucial role in determining the contents, he worked with colleagues as 'a voice among many'. Dawson, *John Knox*, p. 191.

to support his attempts to get Mary's private celebration of Mass forbidden, He asked Calvin 'whether that subjects might put to their hand to suppress the idolatry of their Prince?' Much has been made of the conflict between Knox and the young Queen Mary, but in fact despite these fierce clashes over religion, they were able to cooperate in many matters of state and once acted together as marriage advisers for some of the nobles.[6]

After the Scots Confession, the next major task for Knox and the reformers, was to draw up, for Parliament's approval, a manual for the good order of the Kirk (now the National Church in Scotland) and an outline for the Christian Commonwealth that he hoped it would become, with church and state working together. In 1560 he and colleagues presented to Parliament The First Book of Discipline. Much of it was devoted to education, available to all. It was a strong indication of the Genevan pattern that saw church and state combining within the reformed Christian framework, not just a set of rules for control or even punishment (though at all too many times it was that) but as a manual for church organisation and Christian education.[7]

It declared that to 'Promote the moral culture of every child and the highest good of the community; schools were held to be necessary to establish the Reformed faith.' Schools were to be established in every parish, with schoolmasters appointed by the Kirk, who would teach 'grammar and the Latin tongue' and work with the minister or a lay reader, whose task in this regard was 'take care over the children and youth of the parish' and instruct them in the Reformed Christian faith. Then followed a pattern to establish colleges in every town where the arts, 'at least logic and rhetoric together with the tongues', should be taught.

Above all this document was intended to be a manual, not just for the Kirk, but for what in the centuries after, and in the minds of influential later churchmen such as Thomas Chalmers, was envisioned

---

6. Dawson, *John Knox*, pp. 86-87, 139-40. The issue of resistance to an unjust ruler (or a heretical one) was discussed with Calvin, who advised caution and cited Romans 13 on 'obedience' to divinely appointed rulers, but admitted 'passive disobedience' was permissible. Knox went a great deal further and supported radical plans for a revolution against Mary Tudor in England in 1554.
7. The vision for education in a reformed Scottish nation applied in another cultural context, the African one, is explored by Professor Graham Duncan, 'John Knox and Education', HTS Theological Studies, Vol. 3, No 3 (University of Pretoria 2017). Not paginated - Open Access.

as 'the Godly Commonwealth' that was Knox's vision for a Reformed Scotland. Although the freedom from the constrictions of the alliance of church and state in medieval Scotland was one of the attractions in Reformed Protestantism, Calvin's Geneva saw a different yet equally restrictive alliance, between ministers and magistrates, rather than bishops and kings. The Scots Confession and Book of Discipline, however, allowed some freedom of dissent, and within the 'Godly Commonwealth' more recognition was given to individual expression.

Scottish and Transatlantic Legacy

Oliver Cromwell appropriated the title of 'Commonwealth' into his government of England, and clearly the Puritan tradition that led to many of the early settlements in North America held to that ideal, and to a freedom to establish such a rule, having fled in the seventeenth century from religious persecution in England. History is always a complex web of cause and effect and it is an irony that many of those whose lives were in mortal danger or who laboured under severe repression in Europe were not slow to practise genocide on other so-called 'heathen' original inhabitants, and to make chattels of those who crossed the ocean from Africa and their descendants.

John Knox died over two centuries before America broke away from what the colonists there, or a majority of them, saw as the tyranny of rule from Britain, and well before the enforced exodus of people from Africa in chains reached the flood that it would become in the eighteenth century. Knox was in no position to offer a theological response to chattel slavery. For those nineteen months between 1547 and 1549 he had tasted a similar experience as a rower on a French ship. The captives were chained by leg irons to their bench and when they went ashore they were denied shoes to prevent the success of any attempts to escape. The whip was used to ensure the level of production, and the food provided was inadequate to sustain them. Knox apparently made little mention of his time in captivity, but it had a serious effect on his health and throughout the rest of his life he suffered from digestive problems.[8] Cynics might allege that it accounted for his short temper brought on by dyspepsia.

There is no doubt that one of his enduring legacies were the plan, later carried forward by his successors, for universal education, whose gradual implementation in the nation long after Knox's death in

---

8. Dawson, *John Knox,* p. 53.

1572 made Scotland in later centuries one of the leading countries in Europe both in literacy and in knowledge of the scriptures. His own passion for the combination of education and evangelism to reach the humblest as much as the most elevated in the land was caught in places and centuries far from his own.

That vision and knowledge of the Christian faith and the scriptures could be easily perverted and used to justify so much human behaviour that was destructive. There was a coldness about the Calvinist legacy in Scotland, a harsh and dictatorial aspect to it, and all too often it was appropriated to justify some cruel and pitiless practices that were the antithesis of the master that adherents claimed to follow. Knox was a paradoxical man, perhaps reflecting the burgeoning Calvinist faith that he embraced, and in which he died. But despite that, and perhaps because of the fighting spirit in the man and his passion for the spread of the Christian faith, he was to leave in Scotland and amongst the farflung inheritors of his legacy, a desire to make the scriptures and other learning the means of and the tools for a new society, and for the salvation of souls. For those who needed to exercise total control over the lives of other men and women, such seeds through education could lead to a very profound threat to their domination.

Chapter 2

New World Presbyterians – Slavery and Caution

It's shocking to human nature that any Race of Mankind and their Posterity, should be sentenced to perpetual Slavery; nor in justice can we think otherwise of it, that they are thrown amongst us to be a scourge one day or another for our sins; and as Freedom to them must be as dear as to us, what a scene of horror must it bring about.

—Darien Petition to Governor General George Oglethorpe of Georgia 1739

Slavery and Scots in the Early Decades of Settlements

In the early eighteenth century Scottish Highlanders began to emigrate in large numbers to the American colonies. In the main poverty drove them to it, but it was also a promised opportunity for a freer life. This was not yet the time of the infamous 'Clearances' when landlords, many of whom were absentees in the south of England, decided that the introduction of sheep was a more profitable investment than the rents of tenant farmers. The first Jacobite rising in 1715 had failed, but it was a few years before the second one ended at Culloden in 1745, bringing the Highlands under harsh military rule. The Act of Union of Scotland with England in 1707, though not a popular measure amongst many Scots, nonetheless had given merchants and settlers access to the colonies of North America.

And so a group of Highlanders found their way to settling in southwest Georgia in the mid 1730s. Their area of the colony was named Darien, an unfortunate title, and a throwback to the disastrous attempt in the late seventeenth century at colonising part of the Isthmus of Panama, whose investment bankrupted the nation. Georgia was unique at that time in excluding slavery, not so much on moral grounds, but through the belief, enshrined in the 1735 Act, that slavery posed a danger to security, and would be easy prey in the hands of the nearby Spanish colonists in Florida, who had already helped to foment a rebellion of enslaved men and women in New York and Carolina.

The Darien Petition of 1739 to Governor General Oglethorpe of Georgia has been hailed as a humanitarian document, but the majority of the arguments were more concerned with economics than ethics. The petitioners feared that, although the lifting of the ban on slavery (which happened in 1750) might well enhance the profits of large landowners, the debt incurred in buying and maintaining enslaved people would lead to bankruptcy among small subsistence farmers such as themselves. Although Oglethorpe had declared that a colony dedicated to relieving the distressed of Europe, should not then be involved in the enslaving of free Africans, he himself owned slaves in Carolina and John Mackintosh Bain, the leading petitioner, was later himself to be the 'owner' of eight enslaved people.[1]

Twenty seven years after that petition, the thirteen American states were about to take up arms against the British Empire in making their own bid for freedom from its control. The word 'freedom' was to be liberally used, not least as a basic human right in the years ahead. Yet it would be another three years before Vermont became the first of the states to explicitly ban slavery. In Britain itself, that prohibition would not come until 1834, although in 1778 Scotland's Court of Session in a key case concerning an enslaved man from Jamaica, Joseph Knight, had given judgement by seven votes to four that 'the state of slavery is not recognised by the laws of this kingdom' (Scotland) and the decision was to 'repel the masters' claim to perpetual service.'[2]

---

1. Harvey H. Jackson, 'The Darien Anti-Slavery Petition of 1739 and the Georgia Plan', *The William and Mary Quarterly*, Vol. 34 (Oct. 1977), pp. 618-31.
2. *Caledonian Mercury*, 17 Jan 1778.

Duncan Rice, the Aberdeen-born historian, once wrote 'Eighteenth century Scotland is an extraordinary case of a small country that developed a heavy economic commitment to slavery at the very time when its intelligentsia were vehemently criticising it'. More recently, Scotland's deep involvement at every aspect of the slave trade and plantation slavery has been liberally recognised, but the evidence was there for a very long time. In 1775 the Jamaican slave-owner and historian Edward Long estimated that one-third of the white population of Jamaica, by far the largest slave island in the West Indies, came from 'Northern Britain', and were there as plantation owners, overseers of enslaved people, doctors, lawyers and administrators. The Scottish linen industry benefited greatly from exports of rough cloth for enslaved people in the Caribbean. Glasgow's wealth in the eighteenth century was built on sugar, tobacco and cotton, and Scotland's bard, Robert Burns, who wrote the poignant 'Slaves Lament' had a passage booked to a job on a plantation before his fortunes at home changed.[3]

Even the influence of the Scottish Enlightenment and the teaching of anti-slavery sentiments in universities was not a one-way direction. Giant intellectual figures such as Adam Smith argued for better management of the enslaved to ensure production, and David Hume accepted the assumptions that black people could never achieve anything. Scotland contributed disproportionally to the anti-slavery cause, sending to Parliament in 1792 over one-third of all the petitions from the United Kingdom and Ireland calling for an end to the slave trade. Many of the key figures in the anti-slavery movement were Scots. The Edinburgh lawyer Henry Brougham, later to be Lord Chancellor of England, brought his legal brilliance to bear on it. Zachary Macaulay, son of a manse and later to be editor of the influential *Anti-Slavery Reporter*, and Aberdeen-educated James Stephen, architect of anti-slavery legislation in Parliament, were all native Scots. Yet many of those active in anti-slavery hid this from their relatives in the colonies,

---

3. C. Duncan Rice, *The Scots Abolitionists 1833-1861* (Baton Rouge, LA: University of Louisiana Press, 1981), p. 19.
Iain Whyte, *Scotland and the Abolition of Black Slavery 1756-1838* (Edinburgh: Edinburgh University Press, 2006) pp. 42-56. T.M.Devine (ed.), *Recovering Scotland's Past: The Caribbean Connection* (Edinburgh: Edinburgh University Press, 2015), pp 235-36.

and those who were making their money through slavery were often careful not to reveal the details in their correspondence home.[4]

The Irreconcilable Dilemma

The Founding Fathers of the new United States are prime examples of this uncomfortable disconnection. The author of the Declaration of Independence, Thomas Jefferson (1743-1826) insisted on the insertion of the phrase 'all men are created equal'. He wrote and spoke against slavery, and attempted in Congress in 1784 to ban the slave trade. Nonetheless he owned hundreds of enslaved men and women and only emancipated three of them in his lifetime, and five by his death. James Madison (1751-1836) proposed, in the drafting of the Constitution, that minorities should be protected, but enslaved people should be counted as three-fifths of a human being. He acknowledged the immorality of slavery, and thought it wrong to infer in the Constitution that there could be 'property in men', yet was more concerned to avoid the social upheaval that abolition might cause.

George Washington (1732-99) expressed reservations over slavery all his life and told a British visitor in 1797 that 'nothing but the rooting out of slavery' could perpetuate 'the existence of our union'. As President he signed legislation that banned slavery in the North West Territories in 1789, but did not free those already enslaved. Washington was deeply influenced by Phillis Wheatley, the African American poet, whom he invited to his house, but he not only owned over 200 enslaved people but was known to sanction excessive disciplinary treatment towards them.

Unlike some other denominations such as the Methodists and Quakers, Presbyterians in the years before the Revolution did not have many black members, and chose to stand aside from general condemnation. But one prominent Congregationalist, who was deeply influenced by Calvinism, provided a clear call for abolition of slavery at the outbreak of the Revolutionary War. Revd Samuel Hopkins (1721-1803), a Yale graduate ministering in Rhode Island, addressed the members of the Continental Congress and Representatives of the thirteen colonies, calling upon them to free all their slaves, whom he referred to as 'our brethren and children', and argued that it was

---

4. Whyte, *Scotland and the Abolition of Black Slavery*, pp. 57-62, 99, 103, 117-36.

in the interest of America to do so. His message was controversial. He himself had 'owned' an enslaved man briefly in Massachusetts and Newport, Rhode Island, was an important port for the slave trade. Hopkins has been described as 'the most visible advocate the blacks had in New England during the eighteenth century and their most consistent protagonist'.[5] New England itself was predominantly Calvinist at this time, and its theological pattern of strict adherence to that tradition and zeal for evangelism led it to be known rather clumsily as 'Hopkinsianism'.

Hopkins and his colleague in Newport, Ezra Stiles, devised a project to train a group of African Americans to be missionaries in Africa. His first recruits were the enslaved Bristol Yamma and the free John Quamine, members of his church. He raised enough money to send the two men to college at Princeton, and in a report sent out to well-wishers in April 1776 Hopkins stated that they had 'made such proficiency, and are, such as qualified for the mission proposed, that they would enter it directly, were there opportunity to send them to Africa'.[6]

Hopkins was in contact with Granville Sharp, the pioneer British abolitionist, and Zachary Macaulay, then acting Governor of the 'Free' British settlement in Sierra Leone, but his zealous plans never materialised. John Quamine died in the war, and Bristol Yamma in 1793. The whole issue of black colonisation in Africa became, decades later, a hugely contested issue on which both blacks and whites were deeply divided within their communities. However there is no doubt of Hopkins' sincerity, and no evidence that he acted from racist motives, although he despaired of the possibility that blacks and whites could live together in a single society. In his pamphlet *A Discourse on the Slave Trade and the History of the Africans* he wrote:

> It is a very great wonder and owing to an extraordinary divine intervention, in which we may say that God goes out of his common way, that any of them should think favourably of Christianity or embrace it … they have imbibed the deepest prejudices against it from the treatment they have

---

5. Lawrence N. Jones, *African Americans and the Christian Churches 1619-1860* (Cleveland, OH: Pilgrim Press, 2007), p. 56.
6. Thomas Hopkins, *The Works of Thomas Hopkins* (Boston: Tract Society, 1852, Vol. 1), p. 13.

received from professed Christians; prejudices which most of them are by their circumstances restrained from expressing, while they are fixed in the strongest degree in their minds.[7]

Early Southern Presbyterians and Scottish Influences

One of the earliest and most prominent churches in the South was the First Presbyterian in Charleston, South Carolina, founded in 1731, and known more familiarly as the Scots Presbyterian Church or the Scots Kirk. Many of its ministers were trained in Edinburgh and were products of the Scottish Enlightenment.[8] Amongst them was Alexander Hewat (1740-1824). He became the minister of First Presbyterian in 1763, and immediately began, as a diversion, to study the history of Carolina and Georgia. In it he attempted to be fair to different religious and political perspectives, but his writing burns with passion over what he called the 'horrid and inhuman practice of slavery'. 'Every candid and impartial man', he wrote, 'must confess that it is atrocious and unjustifiable in every light in which it is viewed, and turns merchants into a band of robbers.'

He had some bitter criticism of the failure of his own branch of Christianity to care for the spiritual and intellectual needs of enslaved people. 'To keep the minds of human creatures' he wrote, 'under clouds of darkness, neither disciplined by reason or regulated by religion, is a reproach to the name of Protestants, especially in a land of Christian light and liberty', remarking wryly that even Catholics pitied 'the miserable conditions of negroes living among the American colonies'.[9]

---

7. Ibid. pp. 256-57.
8. The Scottish Enlightenment was a movement from the mid-eighteenth century marking a shift in intellectual awareness from accepted religion to reasoned examination of various disciplines. It included both churchmen and sceptics, and was reflected in the philosophy of leading academics and philosophers.
9. Alexander Hewat, *An Historical Account of the Rise and Progress of the Colonies of South Carolina and Georgia*, Vol. 1 (London, 1779), pp. 75-82, 355. Cited by Erskine Clarke, *Our Southern Zion* (Tuscaloosa, AL: University of Alabama, 1996), pp 70-73.

Hewat had been influenced by William Robertson (1721-93), Principal of Edinburgh University, and the leading figure in the Moderate Party in the Church of Scotland. Moderates were the strong upholders of tradition and the established order, and were delineated from the Popular Party which advocated a more evangelical and missionary approach. Hewat has been described as 'a conservative Tory who loved order, believed in a hierarchical structure of society, and abhorred any movement that might be socially subversive'.[10] Hardly an ideal background for fiercely opposing slavery in a city, and a congregation, which had a strong vested interest in it. Yet William Wilberforce (1759-1833) commended his preaching on the evils of slavery as of the highest support to the cause. Moreover many of the leading figures in the British abolition movement such as Wilberforce and Macaulay were Tories, and stout defenders of many measures at home to maintain social status and prevent radical political change. Hewat's writings, published in 1789 in London, fiercely echoed their basic convictions over the denial of humanity and religious rights in treating human beings as property. This complex and perhaps contradictory system of Presbyterian values in the end led him to leave Charleston and return to Britain, when the American Revolution broke out in 1776.

Church Courts and Temporising Resolutions

In 1787 the Presbyterian Synod of New York and Philadelphia voted to strongly to approve 'the general principles in favour of universal liberty, that prevail in America, and of the interest which many States have taken in promoting the abolition of slavery'. The Committee which drew up the recommendations declared that 'the creator of the world having made of one flesh all the children of men, it becomes them as members of the same family, to consult and promote each other's happiness'. Furthermore it recommended that 'the blessings of equal freedom' be extended 'to every part of the human race'.

There was some reservation before the adoption of this recommendation. It went on to warn of the dangers to society of 'men, introduced from a servile state to a participation of all the privileges of a civil society without a proper education and with previous habits

---

10. Ibid.

of industry'. They then advised members of the church who owned slaves to prepare them for freedom, permitting them, where possible, to buy their freedom, and urged 'all people under their care to use the most prudent measure, consistent with the interest and the state of civil society ... to procure, eventually, the final abolition of slavery in America'.[11]

That was to become a familiar position of many Presbyterian churchmen in the South this time. Few would not, in the last analysis, argue against the proposition that slavery was an unfortunate product of human sin, but the postponement of any steps towards its abolition was an attempt to hold different factions the church together, and effectively to ensure its continuation until the ultimate conflagration of civil war.

There were spasmodic attempts to engage with the possibility of change. In 1794 the Transylvania Presbytery which covered the State of Kentucky, instructed its members who held any who were enslaved to prepare them for 'eventual freedom'.[12]

The 1818 Presbyterian General Assembly produced the strongest statement from that denomination the issue. 'We consider', ran the deliverance:

> The voluntary enslaving of one part of the human race by another, as a gross violation of the most precious and sacred rights of human nature, as utterly inconsistent with the law of God, and as totally irreconcilable with the spirit and principles of the Gospel of Christ, which enjoins that 'all things whatsoever ye would that men should do to you, do ye even so to them.'[13]

Not content simply to emphasise this principle, the Assembly continued: 'It is manifestly the duty of all Christians who enjoy the light of the present day ... as speedily as possible to efface this blot on our

---

11. Jones, *African Americans and the Churches*, pp. 56-57. A Synod in Presbyterian Church government is a higher court that includes a collection of Presbyteries.
12. Lacey.K,.Ford, *Deliver us from Evil: The Slavery Question in the Old South* (Oxford: Oxford University Press, 2009), p. 42.
13. Robert Handy, *A Christian America: Protestant Hopes and Historical Reality* (Oxford: Oxford University Press, 1984) p. 54.

religion, and to obtain the complete abolition of slavery through Christendom and, if possible, throughout the world.' As before, the Assembly warned against the dangers of immediate emancipation, but this time cautioned against 'using that as a cover for the love or practice of slavery, or a pretence for not using efforts that are lawful and practical to extinguish the evil'.

Although this seemed to be an unambiguous statement, the proposer, Revd Ashbel Green, President of Princeton College, who was to emancipate his own enslaved people, stated that 'slaves were not properly prepared for such a radical move' an argument that would be used to maintain slavery and the very cover that the Assembly warned against.[14]

Even the resolutions of the 1818 General Assembly were watered down by an starkly racist overture on African Americans that was accepted at the gathering the next year: 'In the distinction and indelible marks of their color and the prejudice of the people, an insuperable obstacle has been placed to the execution plan to elevate their character and placing them on a footing with the brethren of the same common family.'[15] Lawrence Jones in his survey of African American churches commented on this declaration of 1819:

> In yoking its view of the Africans with the prejudices of the people and concluding that these facts together constituted an insuperable obstacle to change, the Presbyterian Church gave voice to the majority that has articulated the racial policy of the American religious establishment throughout most of its history.[16]

The Moderator that year was Revd John Holt of Virginia. In 1827 he wrote a letter to a friend which encapsulated the dilemma that so many felt. He declared that slavery was 'the greatest evil in our country except whiskey', and that 'it is my ardent prayer that we may be delivered from it'. Yet he continued, 'The reason why I am so strenuously opposed to any movement by ministers of religion is

---

14. *Minutes of the General Assembly of the Presbyterian Church in the United States 1789-1820* (Philadelphia:Presbyterian Board, 1847).
15. Ibid 1819.
16. Jones, *African Americans and the Churches*, p. 7.

this. I am convinced that anything we can do will injure religion, and retard the march of public opinion in relation to slavery.'[17]

Over the years to come the General Assembly, in its attempts to hold together Presbyteries and Synods in the face of calls from some of the Presbyterian family overseas, with the encouragement of American abolitionists, refused to deny membership and communion to those who 'owned' any enslaved men and women. Between 1843 and 1847 great pressure was exerted within and outside the new Free Church of Scotland, which had split from the Church of Scotland, not to accept money from and refuse fellowship with Presbyterian churches that admitted 'slave-owners' to membership. The Free Church refused to do so, but pressed the Presbyterian Church in America to condemn slavery. Irish Presbyterians for a time cut off contact with their American counterparts until they were prepared to take action on their own members.[18]

In 1845 the 'Old School' General Assembly declared that there were obligations on masters and servants, and that masters should remember that 'their master is also in heaven'. But with that rather muted reminder the Assembly continued: 'That the General Assembly was originally organised, and has such continued, the bond of union in the Church upon the conceded principle that the existence of domestic slavery, under the circumstances that it is found in the Southern part of the country, is no bar to Christian Communion'.[19]

This was passed by 168 votes to 13. The next year, almost to convince themselves, the Assembly agreed that the Church has always held and uttered substantially the same sentiments on the subject. In 1849 without a division, the Assembly voted that it was inexpedient and improper for it to attempt or propose methods of emancipation. That position remained until 1861.

---

17. *American National Biography* (Oxford: Oxford University Press 1988) Vol 11, pp. 185-86.
18. Iain Whyte, *'Send Back the Money' The Free Church of Scotland and American Slavery* (Cambridge: James Clark, 2012).
19. In 1837 there was a split between the 'Old School' of Presbyterianism, loyal to traditional Calvinism and led by Charles Hodge, later President of Princeton 1851-78 and the 'New School', keen on evangelism and revival in which Samuel Hopkins took a prominent part. The two were crucially divided on the issue of slavery which the 'New School' wished to see abolished.

New World Presbyterians – Slavery and Caution

At the outbreak of the American Civil War the final breach between North and South Presbyterians became inevitable. Those in the Synod of South Carolina meeting in December 1860 who wished to avoid this argued that the General Assembly of 1845 had denied any authority to make any laws on slavery. But the Synod seceded from the church, and exactly a year later the General Assembly of the new Presbyterian Church in the Confederacy declared not only that the slave system had generally proved to be 'kindly and benevolent' but that it provided 'real effective discipline' to a people who could not be elevated in any other way, and that slavery was the black man's 'normal condition'.[20]

A Small Denomination Takes a Firm Stand

Despite this overall Presbyterian accommodation to slavery, recent scholarship has unearthed a more uncompromising attitude in a small Presbyterian denomination, the Reformed Presbyterian Church in the United States. With a membership that, even by the middle of the nineteenth century amounted to around 3-4 per cent of the whole Presbyterian family, its contribution and its consistency in its opposition to slavery mark it out alongside a denomination at the other end of the theological spectrum, the Quakers, or Society of Friends.

The Reformed Church's roots came from the Covenanters, those who in 1643 signed an alliance with the English Parliament to ensure that the Reformed practice had precedence in Scotland. King Charles II on his accession revoked it in favour of Episcopalianism, which was imposed on Scotland in the mid seventeenth century. Scottish and Irish Covenanters were to flee persecution in the years following, and a considerable number came to the United States. The first presbytery of the Reformed Church in America was founded in Pennsylvania in 1774.

Not surprisingly the opposition to state tyranny ensured that these new immigrants from the Covenanting tradition were in the main strong supporters of the American Revolution. Some historians consider that equally the seeds of active anti-slavery had also been planted in their time in Scotland. That is less certain, but soon after the new nation had been established, the Reformed Church in

---

20. Eugene Genovese, *Roll, Jordan, Roll: The World the Slaves Made* (New York: Pantheon, 1974), p. 187.

America called for a day of public fasting in repentance on slavery. They declared that:

> That abominable species of murder, even enslaving thousands of fellow creatures for life and their posterity without end, and degrading them below the brutes, is now reduced to a regular system, and seems by long prescription, to brave a remedy... Oh! America, what hast thou to account for, both to God and man, on the head of slavery alone? Alas when shall God arise for the cries of the oppressed.[21]

These fine words, or similar, had of course been uttered many times by churches with little effect. Revd Alexander McLeod, who came from the island of Mull in Scotland, where his father was a Church of Scotland minister, had early in the nineteenth century been called to two Reformed congregations in New York City. As a condition for accepting this he demanded and obtained an agreement that no 'slave-owners' would be permitted to take communion within the Reformed Presbytery. Incredibly two ministers were commissioned to take this ruling to South Carolina and perhaps even more remarkably three Reformed churches in South Carolina acceded to it, with few leaving the congregation. In 1801 Revd William Martin, a leading Covenanter in Ireland and America, was charged with having sold a slave. He was deposed from the ministry, though the charge was also combined with one of public drunkenness.

In 1802 McLeod published a sermon 'Negro Slavery Unjustifiable' in which he attacked the institution. Others had done this from a liberal perspective but McLeod, in company with his church, was a biblical literalist. He attacked the 'curse of Ham' (Genesis 9) as erroneous in its justification of the treatment of Africans, and he drew on the Sermon on the Mount and the injunction in Matthew's Gospel to treat others as you wish to be treated 'for this is the law and the

---

21. William J. Roulson, 'The Reformed Church and Anti-Slavery in Nineteenth-Century America' in William Harrison Taylor and Peter C. Messer (eds.), *Faith and Slavery in the Presbyterian Diaspora* (Bethlehem: Leigh High University Press, 2006) p. 154. I am indebted to Dt Roulston of the Ulster Historical Association for his research on this little known aspect of a Presbyterian church and slavery.

prophets'.[22] Other Reformed Presbyterians used publications to attack slavery – the *Evangelical Witness* and *The Reformed Presbyterian* carried many articles and Reformed ministers contributed to William Lloyd Garrison's celebrated paper of the anti-slavery movement, *The Liberator*.

For a tiny, and theologically conservative denomination, the Reformed Church in America gave practical expression to their principles far beyond their numbers. Many ministers and members were involved in that remarkable network the 'Underground Railroad' that enabled thousands of enslaved people to escape from slave states to the North and to Canada after slavery was abolished in the British Empire in 1834. Reformed meeting houses often served as 'stations' on the 'railroad' where the self-liberated were sheltered and directed on safe paths. Many in the Church agreed with William Lloyd Garrison that the American Constitution was fundamentally flawed. Some took this view further by advocating armed resistance to slavery. Some Covenanters even supported those who embraced armed resistance. Revd A.A. Milligan of Pennsylvania 'an humble pastor' of a congregation of people known as Scotch Covenanters', supported John Brown in his rebellion in 1859 and called his execution 'judicial murder'. Revd J.R.W. Sloan in New York regarded Brown as a 'martyr-hero', and helped to raise funds for his family.[23] By the mid-nineteenth century there were few Covenanting congregations in the South, and although many ministers such as McLeod called for the immediate abolition of slavery, others took a 'gradualist' approach (a split that was to be found in the British Anti-Slavery Movement in the early 1830s).

Long before then it had become impossible for abolitionists to minister as Presbyterians in the South. As early as 1796 the Presbytery of South Carolina refused to ordain Revd James Gillilad unless he agreed not to preach against slavery. He then moved to Ohio. In 1815 Revd George Bourne in West Virginia questioned whether Presbyterian slaveholders could remain in the church. The following year he published a strong critique of the churches, *The Book and Slavery Irreconcilable*, which demanded total and immediate emancipation. After a trial by Presbytery, the General Assembly reversed

---

22. Samuel Brown Wylie. *Memoir of Alexander Mcleod* (New York: C.Scribner,1855) p. 51.
23. Roulston, 'The Reformed Church and Anti-Slavery' pp. 153-165.

the decision to expel him from the ministry. but he left for the North fearing that his life was in danger. In 1818 the General Assembly upheld the earlier trial and his licence was removed from him.[24]

John Rankin of Ripley (1793-1886)

Today the manse of Revd John Rankin, Presbyterian minister in Ripley, Ohio, is a national monument. It stands on a hill above the Ohio river, over which many enslaved people moved from the Kentucky side and found shelter and protection from the Rankin family, who often hid them from slave-catchers. It was a key station on the Underground Railroad. Rankin was brought up in Tennessee, but had to leave the state in 1817 for anti-slavery preaching and then terminated a ministry in Kentucky after attacks by a mob on his school for enslaved children. In 1822 he arrived in Ripley. Henry Ward Beecher (husband of Harriet Beecher Stowe, the author of *Uncle Tom's Cabin*) may have taken poetic licence when he was asked after the Civil War that ended slavery, who it was who abolished it, and answered 'Revd John Rankin and his sons' but it was a fitting, if flowery tribute to one Presbyterian minister who stood firm and rescued many from enslavement.[25]

---

24. David Brion Davis: *The Problem of Slavery in the Age of Revolution 1770-1823* (Ithaca, NY: Cornell University Press), p. 201.
25. Ann Hagedorn, *Beyond the River: The Untold Story of Heroes of the Underground Railroad* (New York: Simon and Schuster (2001) p. 274.

Chapter 3

The Dilemmas of Some Princetonians

Oh that it had been my lot to have spent my days where slavery was unknown. To speak as a Christian I really fear some heavy judgement awaits us on that score.'
—David Ramsay to Benjamin Rush. Charleston, 1775

The American religious revival of the mid-eighteenth century, known as 'The Great Awakening', led to a deep concern for evangelism and missionary work.[1] This took various forms, from whites who could hardly ignore enslaved and free black people in taking seriously the Gospel imperative. In some cases it was closely allied to colonialism, and in others it became emmeshed in selective religious education that focussed on obedience. But at its best, notable Presbyterians in America, some of whom were highly influential in the new nation, embraced the Reformers' passion of linking education with Christian evangelism. Perhaps nowhere was this more strikingly seen than in the College of New Jersey, later to become Princeton. It became known as the College for Presbyterians, although its students included those of other traditions.

---

1. The Great Awakening was a movement for religious revival and enthusiasm in the late eighteenth century with regular peaks up to the campaigns of Dr Billy Graham in the mid-twentieth.

Samuel Davies (1723-1761) 'Apostle' to the Enslaved

In 1753 Samuel Davies travelled to Britain with a colleague to raise funds for the College of New Jersey. This was at the request of the College Trustees at a time when urgent financial needs required a persuasive advocate, and Davies was highly regarded as an evangelist. He accompanied another minister and fellow Trustee, Gilbert Tennant, with the goal of raising £300. The enormous sum of £3,000 was collected on this trip, and enabled the College to move from Newark to Princeton. Six years later Davies was invited to become its President, a position he held for a short time until his death in early 1761.

Davies was born in Pennsylvania of poor parents, and had only a basic education. At 15 he became deeply influenced by the revivalist minister Samuel Blair, who took him under his wing. Blair not only founded a college in the state, but was one of the first Trustees of the New Jersey College. After training in the classics and theology, Davies was ordained, and sent to minister to seven Presbyterian churches in Virginia, where he had a passion for evangelism of both enslaved and free blacks. He castigated both his fellow clergy and the 'owners' of enslaved people for their lack of enthusiasm to extend evangelism towards those human beings that they held in servitude. In a sermon in 1754 he claimed that the duty of a Christian was to 'propagate religion among the heathen' and he earnestly recommended that masters take seriously their responsibilities for religious education of those whom they held in slavery.[2]

A number of Presbyterian theologians and educators in the South would later emphasise the sacred duties of masters to seek the salvation of the souls of those they held captive, but Davies was a pioneer in his denomination. When he addressed 'slave-owners', he emphasised that all were destined for immortality, and that the distinctions of rank or race had no place beyond the grave. He made a plea to all involved in enslavement: Will you not labor to make this land of slavery a land

---

2. *American National Biography*, Vol. 6, pp 160-62. Helpful scholarly work on Davies is to be found in a paper from Isabela Morales, 'Samuel Davies', Princeton and Slavery Project, Princeton.edu/stories/Samuel-Davies.

of special liberty to them ... as a reward for the fruits of their labors which you enjoy?'³

To minister in the South, albeit the Upper South of Virginia, at this time was almost by definition to reach an accommodation with slavery. Davies himself 'owned' several people, two of whom were given to him by parishioners in Virginia. He asked to be judged by his treatment of them, and in a sermon to a group of enslaved people in 1755 challenged those who heard, to let them say whether or not he treated them kindly or not. Lawrence Jones recognised the constraints that Davies was under, and claimed that he never saw slavery as 'a positive good' even if it exposed African Americans to the potential benefits of the Gospel, an all too familiar argument to conveniently bridge the gap between guilt and pragmatism over the existing situation.⁴

Davies spent energy, resources (which he gathered from well-wishers and overseas contacts) and, no doubt, some of his modest stipend, in gathering Bibles and other religious literature to make available to enslaved people. Virginia did not then have, as many slave states were later to adopt, a legal ban on any literature for those in slavery, with draconian penalties for them and any who taught them literacy. It may be that African Americans were more interested in access to books than conversion, seeing this as a way of glimpsing a world beyond their chains, but Davies fully embraced the Reformed tradition of using learning, especially religious education, as an essential tool towards building up a godly community.

In 1751 he wrote in a letter to a friend:

> There is also a number of Negroes. Sometimes I see a hundred or more among my hearers. I have baptised about forty of them within these three years, upon such profession of faith as I then judged credible. Some of them I fear have apostatised; but others, I trust, will persevere to the end. I have had the satisfying evidence of the sincere piety of several of them, as I ever had from any persons in my life, and their artless simplicity, their passionate aspirations

---

3. Samuel Davies, *The Duties of Masters to their Servants* (Lynchburg, VA: William W. Gray, 1809).
4. Jones, *African Americans and the Churches,* pp. 57-58.

after Christ, their incessant endeavours to know and do the will of God, has charmed me.⁵

To modern eyes this may seem to read as pure sentimentality, even hypocrisy, given that Samuel Davies held back on emancipation. But as one historian is quick to point out, Davies never succumbed to the racist myth that African Americans were incapable of education, still less that they lacked common humanity. In his efforts, he not only laid the foundations for the later development of significant black congregations throughout the Upper South, but he also brought this passion for bringing the Gospel to enslaved people to the students who were briefly under his care at Princeton.⁶

John Witherspoon (1723-1794) – The Conservative Revolutionary

In April 1756 a young man was baptised as James Montgomery in Beith Parish Church, Ayrshire, Scotland. The baptism was not recorded in the parish records. Jamie, as he became known, was 'owned' by Robert Sheddan, who had brought him to Scotland to be trained as a carpenter (or 'joiner' in the more familiar Scots) and, with his price enhanced, planned to sell him back in Virginia. Hearing of the plan, Jamie liberated himself and went to Edinburgh, where he was imprisoned. Sheddan raised an action in Scotland's highest court, the Court of Session, but before judgment could be finally given, Jamie died.⁷

The parish minister who baptised the young Virginian was John Witherspoon, shortly to transfer to St George's Church in Paisley, but who in 1766 travelled to America to assume the Presidency of the College of New Jersey, and ten years later became the only Scot and the only clergyman to sign the American Declaration of Independence.

Witherspoon on 21 April 1756, the day before Montgomery's planned transportation back to America, gave a certificate of Christian character to him stating that he may be received as a member of any Christian Society where Providence shall order him Montgomery's

---

5. Samuel Davies, *Memoir of Reverend Samuel Davies* (Boston: Massachusetts Sabbath School Society, 1832) p. 22.
6. Jones, *African Americans and the Churches*, pp. 59-60.
7. Whyte, *Scotland and the Abolition of Black Slavery*, pp. 14, 15.

master told the judges that he had been reluctant to allow the baptism, in case of 'fancies of freedom which it might instil in the slave' and he argued that the minister in Beith had instructed Montgomery to be obedient to his master and emphasised to him 'again and again that baptism by no means freed him from his servitude'.[8]

When John Witherspoon give Jamie Montgomery a certificate of Christian conduct, he would be well aware that Jamie had already attempted to escape from Sheddan's clutches several times. He had decided to baptise Jamie in the face of reluctance by the master. What use would be such a certificate to a slave? Was the minister at least sympathetic to Montgomery's possible freedom?

Witherspoon was a complex character. A supporter of the evangelical Popular Party of the Church of Scotland, he nonetheless in his philosophical lectures embraced the attitude of the Moderates, who were, for all their political conservatism, more open to new philosophical thinking. In Scotland Witherspoon was fiercely opposed to the Jacobite cause, which challenged the British Hanovarian monarchy, and critical of clergy who took part in politics, yet threw his lot in with the American Revolution at the highest level. In 1774 he published an essay in which he wrote 'we are firmly determined never to submit (to British sovereignty) and do deliberately prefer war with all its horrors, and even extermination itself to slavery, riveted on us and our posterity'.[9]

It would be surprising if John Witherspoon as a young minister ever approved of chattel slavery. If so, he would have been among a tiny minority of churchmen in Scotland. Certainly he believed in an ordered society, but it is doubtful if he would have been as sympathetic to the rights of the master as Robert Sheddan assured the Court of Session was the case. Otherwise what reason would there be for him to issue the certificate to Jamie, not just confirming his baptism, but commending him to others as a good Christian? The plan to return him to Virginia was one that by definition assumed that he would be strictly controlled in his movements.

---

8. Memorial for James Montgomery-Sheddan, 23 July 1756 NAS CS 255/K/2/2, pp. 16, 23, 24.

9. *American National Biography,* Vol. 23, p.706. The Scottish 'Common Sense' philosophy was part of the Scottish Enlightenment's philosophical attitude that valued reason above revelation.

There was however no consistent pattern to Witherspoon's later theoretical attitude to the slavery of others. He relied much on the thinking of the moral philosopher Frances Hutchison (1694-1746), who was an influential figure in the Scottish Enlightenment. Alongside most of the Enlightenment thinkers, Hutcheson saw slavery as undesirable and uncivilised, and wrote strongly about its cruelty, but stopped short of an absolute condemnation by making a number of exceptions. David Brion Davis, the American historian, commented that Hutcheson 'sawed through the conventional rationalisations for slavery' but that his reservations 'leave a somewhat ragged edge'.[10]

There was certainly a 'ragged edge' that came through Witherspoon's published works. A keen follower of John Locke's philosophy of freedom, he could not commit himself to the Englishman's forthright declaration that slavery was 'so vile and miserable an estate of man' that no civilised nation could approve of it. Witherspoon's *Lectures on Moral Philosophy* which he gave to many training for ministry in the Presbyterian tradition, mirrored this combination of Scottish Common Sense philosophy on nature and God, allied with a passion for Calvinist order in church and state, leavened by the insistence by Knox (and Calvin) that unjust rulers could, even must, be resisted, by rebellion if necessary.[11]

Yet the idea of the right of a rebellion by those enslaved was anathema to him. He accepted Locke's reservation that there are circumstances where some could become enslaved by consent, but he went much further. In his *Lectures* Witherspoon asked: 'whether it is lawful to make men or to keep them slaves, slaves without their consent?' It was a question that he might have heard raised in debating circles in Scotland, though being part of the Popular Party in the Kirk he would keep clear of the established Moderates, many of whom would endlessly discuss questions such as these in the new coffee houses in Edinburgh and Glasgow.

Influenced perhaps by the Calvinist doctrine of 'the elect' and predestination, he was to underpin a key theological argument for slavery when he wrote 'in every state there must be some superior and others inferior, and it is hard to fix the degree of subjection that may

---

10. David Brion Davis, *The Problem of Slavery in Western Culture* (Ithaca, NY: Cornell University Press, 1966), p. 377.
11. John Witherspoon, *Lectures on Moral Philosophy* (Princeton: Princeton University Press, 1912), XII, pp. 96-97, 72-74.

fall on the lot of particular person'. Admitting that there were many ways of enslaving others that were unjustified, he added that 'there are also some that are lawful'.[12]

Witherspoon himself owned two enslaved people valued at $200 in the inventory of his property at his death in 1794. As with other leaders of the American revolution, the sacredness of property was a high priority for him. His conservative instincts led him to link the franchise to the ownership of property in the Bill of Rights of 1776 and enslaved people were certainly excluded from this in the new republic. The cry 'No Property in Man' which was heard in England at the time of slavery cases, and which impacted in the crucial decision in Scotland in 1778, was hardly heard in the distinctions between whites and blacks over the Atlantic.

At Princeton Witherspoon had a great deal of influence over the Presbyterian students, some of whom were to hold key professional roles and many to become leading ministers in the church. Quite a few of those were to play a key part in the South. He opened up their thinking about the moral law of God, the ordering of society, consent and contract undergirding its citizens, and their rights as individuals. Some of the liberating effects of Calvinism have often been buried below its restrictive extremes, but Witherspoon encouraged his students in the former, not least by his later record as a pioneer of the American Revolution. By the time that he arrived at Princeton in 1768 there was a strong anti-slavery sentiment amongst the students, and some were active in the fledgling movement to see its abolition. There is no record that the new President gave them any support, but he would encourage them to engage philosophically with moral issues, including the persistent one of whether continuing to enslave people was compatible with the values espoused by the rebellious new nation. When he presented the Virginia Bill of Rights in June 1776 it held the familiar words 'the enjoyment of life and liberty, with the means of acquiring and possessing property'. Although a recent book on him is titled *An Animated Son of Liberty* John Witherspoon's life reflects a very different limited perspective on liberty.[13]

---

12. Ibid., X, pp. 72-74.
13. J. Walter McGinty, *An Animated Son of Liberty* (Bury St Edwards: Arena Books: 2012).

David Ramsay (1749-1815) and Benjamin Rush (1746-1813): The Medical Politicians

A short time before Witherspoon's arrival at Princeton, David Ramsay, the son of Irish Presbyterian immigrants in rural Pennsylvania, graduated from the college. He then undertook studies at Philadelphia's medical school where he qualified as a doctor in 1773, and the next year moved to Charleston, South Carolina, to practise medicine. Ramsay entered politics and served in the South Carolina legislature before and after the Revolutionary War, part of which he spent as a prisoner of the British. Throughout his political life in the State House and Senate he maintained his role as a doctor, and in addition he made a considerable contribution as a historian chronicling the annals of South Carolina and America. He married three times. From his first wife Sabina he inherited indirectly 4 enslaved men and women. His second wife Frances was a daughter of John Witherspoon and his third wife Martha was daughter of Henry Laurens, a very wealthy merchant engaged in the slave trade.[14]

For a young man of 25 arriving in the South to practise medicine it must have been a culture shock and an exposure in a very direct way to the institution of slavery. The family influences played their part, but although he was to engage in extensive correspondence with Witherspoon on moral issues, including slavery, the man whom he regarded as a lifelong mentor was the one to whom he had written the poignant words quoted at the beginning of this chapter, another signatory to the Declaration of Independence, Dr Benjamin Rush.

Rush was three years older than Ramsay and had graduated from Princeton at the young age of 14. His years at the College coincided with the short tenure of Davies as President, who had a great influence on him. After an apprenticeship in medicine in his native Philadelphia, he took further studies at the University of Edinburgh, under the eminent scientist Joseph Black and the medical pioneer William Cullen. Later on as a physician in the Revolutionary War, he took up Cullen's ideas on the influence of the nervous system in all medical conditions. His drive to understand mental illness, and his

---

14. Arthur H. Shaffer, 'Between Two Worlds: David Ramsay and the Politics of Slavery', *Journal of Southern History*, Vol. 50, no. 2, May 1984. pp. 175-96.

campaigning for a more humane approach, earned him the title of 'Father of American Psychiatry'.[15]

On landing at Liverpool in 1766 Rush never forgot the sight of a large number of slave ships in the harbour. In 1773 he wrote a pamphlet *An Address to the Inhabitants of the British Settlements in America, Upon Slave Keeping*. In it he made an uncompromising attack, not just on the slave trade, but on slavery itself. He argued that black people by nature were neither morally or intellectually inferior, and that slavery was 'so foreign to the human mind that the moral faculties, as those of the understanding are debased and rendered torpid by it'.[16]

Yet ambiguity remained even in this forthright abolitionist. In 1784 he helped to found the Pennsylvania Society for the Abolition of Slavery. He also supported the Free African Society, which was the springboard for the first independent African church in Philadelphia. But he owned enslaved men and women, whom he did not free until much later in his life. In an early essay on slavery he affirmed ironically that those who had 'acquired all the low vices of slavery, or who from age or infirmity are unfit to be set at liberty', for the good of society should remain as the property 'of those from whom they contracted those vices and infirmaties'.[17]

Rush was an evangelical Christian, but one whose theological position became more liberal with the years. His roots were Presbyterian, but at different times he was an Anglican, Methodist, and even a Unitarian. He sought to retain his original Calvinism combined with his conviction that all should be able to share in salvation. When he befriended David Ramsay as a senior physician, the younger man must have enjoyed, or perhaps been disturbed by, the theological swings and roundabouts of his mentor. But Rush's views on slavery, capital punishment (which he also opposed) and women's rights continued. Amongst the myriad of involvements were strong support for the Revolution, and his key role as Surgeon General in Washington's Army certainly enhanced his reputation in the eyes of Ramsay.

---

15. *American National Biography*, Vol. 19. pp. 73-75.
16. Benjamin Rush, *An Address to the Inhabitants of the British Settlements in America Upon Slave Keeping* (Philadelphia: J. Dunlap, 1773).
17. Gideon Mailer, 'Between Enlightenment and Evangelicalism: Presbyterian Diversity and American Slavery 1700-1800', in Messer and Taylor (eds.), *Faith and Slavery in the Presbyterian Diaspora* p.56-60.

Benjamin Rush was Ramsay's closest confidant. He strengthened, rather than initiated, the younger man's disgust with slavery. Ramsay had been exposed to philosophical anti-slavery as a student, and to its reality when, as a young medic, he accompanied Rush into poor areas of Philadelphia. It might seem a strange decision therefore when, at Rush's bidding, he sought to establish a medical practice in a key city in the centre of the lower South. Why should he urge his protégé to make a career in Charleston? How could an abolitionist survive in this field, let alone be elected to public office?

The answer to this question lay probably in what many saw as the fluid situation over slavery in the late eighteenth century. Attitudes to slavery in the deep South were not uniform, even from those who were themselves involved in the institution. Just as the slave-owning Fathers of the Revolution had a curious ambivalence over slavery and freedom, so Southern leadership at that time was very uncertain about the future, and deeply divided over the slave trade. Ramsay was to write to Rush that he had 'a firm belief that there will not be a slave in these states fifty years hence'.[18]

At the start of his political career there was an imminent threat of invasion by British troops. Considerable debate took place in the state legislature over whether enslaved people should be given arms to defend the city. Ramsay had various thoughts. Such a plan, he believed, would have to be accompanied with emancipation, otherwise the Africans would simply defect to the British. At a deeper level he believed that the siege and invasion would be in accordance with a divine plan to cleanse America from the sin of slavery. On the practical side he said that it 'would teach the people experimentally the folly of 'accumulating negroes" and that the loss would 'make it necessary to live in a more republican manner'.

'Slave-owners' were hardly disposed to see it that way, and they faced the economic loss involved. Ramsay was more and more looked on with suspicion as a Northerner, and tarred, with some justification, with the accusation of being in league with the abolitionists. After the war was over, he was a strong supporter of the reinstitution of the slave trade, following losses of slaves in the conflict. By 1785 economic factors led to many Carolinians supporting a ban on slave

---

18. David Ramsay to Benjamin Rush, 20 Jun 1779.

trading on the same initial grounds as earlier Scots in Georgia – the need to purchase would incur insupportable debt.

Many Southerners saw the abolition of the slave trade as the thin end of the wedge towards emancipation. Northern abolitionists certainly saw it as a necessary stage, as did Ramsay's third father-in-law, Henry Laurens (1724-1792). The Laurens family wealth had been built up on slavery. Every year in the mid century he had imported thousands of human beings from the West African oast through the station on the Sierra Leone river run by his Scottish friend and son of the manse, Richard Oswald. By this time Laurens, who like Ramsay had been imprisoned for a time by the British, had sought to disengage from slavery, and supported his son-in-law's concern to weaken it through a ban on the trade. Ironically enough when Ramsay married Martha Laurens in 1787, she brought a number of enslaved people with her, and the ownership of lands in South Carolina and Georgia, worked of course by them. Henry Laurens had considerably changed his views on what had built his wealth, and he saw the banning of the slave trade as a step to the ending of it. 'Could I but prevail on my fellow citizens to prohibit further importation', he wrote in 1785, 'happy families will become more general and time will work manumission or a state equal to it.'

With time Ramsay, conscious of his unique position as a Northerner, modified his stance on slavery. His theological understanding, based on a Calvinist background, saw the institution as 'one principal source of vice'. He was influenced by Granville Sharp, the British abolitionist, who taught that God's punishment awaited those who clung to sinful ways, and slaveholding was certainly that. Yet his arguments, perhaps based on a pragmatism that increasingly recognised how little room for manoeuvre he had, were increasingly made on economic rather than moral grounds. In his *History of the American Revolution* he absolved Southerners from responsibility for introducing slavery or for the need to stop it. He recognised that the North, whose climate enabled white people to labour on farms, was in contrast to that of Southern plantations. His attitude to black people swung from the belief in a common humanity to claiming that the differences in the two races made slavery more acceptable a fate for blacks than whites. He fell back on the familiar argument made by British defenders of West Indian slavery, that most enslaved people did not seek emancipation, and that 'the peasantry of few countries enjoy as much of the comforts of life, as the slaves', going on to conclude ludicrously that often life is enjoyed more by the slave than the master'.[19]

Such accommodation in the end did not assist in securing the advancement of Ramsay's political career, and in 1778 he came a poor third in his attempt to represent South Carolina in Congress. The winner accused Ramsay of being 'principled against the true interests of this country ... it is very well known that he is principled against slavery'. It was a turning point for him. By the last decade of the century the debate on slavery itself in the lo South was effectively closed. Modest changes, and even substantial ones such as the suspension of the slave trade from 1787 until 1803, did not alter the fact that emancipation was no longer on the agenda in South Carolina. Ramsay recognised this, although to the end he claimed to his friends that he regarded slavery to be incompatible with republicanism and harmful to both races. Yet he lived in an atmosphere where it had become increasingly key to the economic and social system and when he wrote his famed *History of South Carolina*, not only was it a history of white South Carolina, but he was totally silent on the subject of slavery. And at his death, for all his philosophy on slavery, the enslaved on his land remained in exactly the same position.

---

19. David Ramsay, *History of the American Revolution,* ed. Lester Cohen (Indianapolis: Liberty Fund, 1989). Cited in Peter C. Messer, 'A Blessing or a Curse, Depending on How it is Used: David Ramsay's Presbyterian Anti-Slavery Journey', in Messer and Taylor (eds.), *Faith and Slavery in the Presbyterian Diaspora* .pp. 95-120.

Chapter 4

Rebellion and Reaction

We are free, but the white people here wont let us be so; and the only way is to raise up and fight the whites.
—Denmark Vesey, Charleston, South Carolina, 1822

Whereas the slave Nat, otherwise known as Nat Turner, the contriver and leader of the late Insurrection in Southampton, is still going at large: therefore I, John Floyd, Governor of the Commonwealth of Virginia, offer a reward of five hundred dollars to any person or persons who will apprehend and convey to the jail of Southampton County the said slave Nat.
—Governor John Floyd, 17 September 1831

John Knox for some years had struggled to find justification for resistance to tyrants. John Calvin was ambivalent over this, and tended to be more influenced by the Pauline injunction in his letter to the Romans to submit to the powers that be, who were 'ordained by God'.[1] In 1558 Knox addressed his *Appellation* to the Scottish nobility, whom he saw as agents of God 'to repress the rage and insolence of your kings, whensoever they pretend manifestly God's blessed ordinance'.[2]

---

1. Romans 13:1-2.
2. Dawson. *John Knox*, p. 157.

It has often been said that history is written by the victors. Certainly it overwhelmingly features the powerful and the well to do, and reflects their prejudices and preferences. The history of resistance of enslaved people in the century before emancipation, has both been downplayed to lessen its importance, or fashioned to serve racial interests. It is not without irony that one of the most popular marching songs of the Union Army in the American Civil War was 'John Brown's Song' (known later as 'John Brown's Body') which celebrated, with a kind of martyrdom, the white leader of a rebellion that had followed some equally striking black ones. Brown himself in his speech from the dock recognised the selectiveness of attitudes when he declared that had he interfered 'on behalf of the rich, the powerful, the great army of their friends' and suffering as he had done 'every man would have deemed it an act worthy of reward rather that punishment'.[3]

Alongside the myth of Southern slavery being a benevolent relationship in which the enslaved were satisfied with their lot, was the constant fear, in cities and rural areas, of rebellion. There is evidence that many parts of the South – Virginia, South Carolina, Georgia and Louisiana – saw attempted uprisings which were either real or imagined, since the authorities were quick to seize on any rumours or testimonies of other enslaved people who in other matters held no weight in court cases. Two rebellions (and there were others) were especially significant in the early part of the nineteenth century – those led by Denmark Vesey in 1822 and Nat Turner in 1831.

Denmark Vesey (c.1767-1822) and his 'Plot' – Truth and Fiction

In late June 1822 white and black Charlestonians became very much afraid. The former feared for their lives and property at the hands of the latter, whereas the enslaved and 'free' black Charlestonians feared for increasing restriction on their lives, not just from the white vigilante groups who would think nothing of killing them, but of accusations of insurrection and false testimony that might lead to a judicial death. The reason was the 'discovery' of a plot, under the direction of one of the most uncompromising of Charleston's black citizens, Denmark Vesey.

---

3. John Brown, Charlestown, WV, 2 Dec. 1859.

Vesey had been brought from West Africa in the 1770s to the Caribbean where for a time he worked in Saint-Domingue (shortly after to become Haiti) and as a young man was taken to Charleston and enslaved by Joseph Vesey, a slave trader, sea captain and planter. By an incredible stroke of good fortune, he won $1,500 in the Charleston East Bay lottery, purchased his freedom for $600, and then set up a carpenter's business, leading to extensive contacts within the free black community, at that time numbering nearly 1,500.[4]

In 1817 Denmark Vesey was one of 'three people of color' who were admitted to communion at Second Presbyterian church in Charleston, established six years previously. He had probably been associated with the congregation for some time, since there is no record of his baptism at that time, as there is with the other two. That same year a group of free African American members, disillusioned with the white control of the large black membership of Bethel Methodist Church, formed a branch of the newly founded African Methodist Episcopal Church on Cow Alley in the north of Charleston. It was later named Emmanuel. By the next year Denmark Vesey had become one of its class leaders and effectively associate pastor.

From very early days Vesey refused to accommodate himself to what has been described as the 'mask of obedience as a survival technique' for enslaved and free Charlestonian blacks. A very tall and imposing figure, he was free in his opinions on slavery in taverns and grog shops, and shocked men of both races by his denunciation of the slave system and of racial inferiority. Above all he refused to lower his eyes in the presence of whites but looked them boldly in the face, or, as his biographer put it 'given his great height, stared down at them – in a calculated act of insolence'.[5]

The founding minister in 1816 of Emmanuel AME Zion Church in Charleston was Revd Morris Brown (1770-1849). Denmark Vesey found him too accommodating towards the city's whites, and judged his eloquent sermons to show an unwillingness to engage with the issues of slavery and liberation. This was as hardly surprising, since

---

4. Thomas Higginson, 'Denmark Vesey', *The Atlantic* (June 1861), p. 730. *American National Biography*, Vol. 22, pp. 338-39. The figure is taken from the Charleston records in 1820.
5. Douglas R. Egerton, *He Shall Go Free: The Lives of Denmark Vesey* (Madison, WI: Madison House, 1999), p. 99.

it would have fatally imperilled the already tenuous situation of the black church.

Vesey's class teaching held no such restrictions. He embraced revolutionary theology. Yet unlike many leaders of oppressed people, who found inspiration in the life of Jesus, he embraced what one of his colleagues described as a vision 'in the stern and Nemesis- like God of the Old Testament' which gave inspiration toward 'a day of vengeance and retribution'. In the Bible class Vesey focussed on the book of Exodus and on aspects that many white Christians were determined to hide from enslaved and free blacks. The story of the liberation from Egypt of the Hebrew slaves he grasped as the narrative that would inspire and inflame the oppressed for revolution.

Daniel Vesey met the traditional theological justification for slavery in the Old Testament by exploring it further and turning it around. The law of Moses held the divine command to release a Hebrew slave after seven years, and this gave, for Vesey, not just a warrant, but an obligation, on all enslaved people to rise up after that time. He particularly dwelt on enslavement as a capital offence, as stated in Exodus 21:16. 'he that stealeth a man and selleth him, or if he be found in his hand, shall be put to death.' Interpreting Jerusalem as the city of God's favour, he quoted the book of the prophet Zechariah which predicted the destruction of all peoples ranged against her, and in the book of Joshua the story of the righteous destruction of Jericho with the slaughter of all men, women and livestock.[6]

Vesey has been described as having a 'utopian vision' that reimagined a new social reality. His uncompromising use of the Old Testament broke any acceptance of the status quo, and demanded that things could be different, and that God intended them to be different. He took the longing for freedom which had been channelled towards a heavenly goal, that was relatively unthreatening to white power, and gave the enslaved a concrete earthly and immediate one, the destruction of the present order in Charleston and their escape from bondage.[7]

One of his closest disciples, who was with many others to suffer execution with him in July 1822, was an enslaved carpenter Jack Purcell (known as 'Gullah' Jack) whose original home was either

---

6. Ibid., pp. 114-15.
7. Erskine Clarke, *Our Southern Zion*, (Tuscaloosa, Al: University of Alabama Press 1996), p. 123.

Zanzibar or Angola. Jack was influential in the black community, and had a reputation for being invulnerable. He was a magician and a traditional African priest, using a crab's claw and other items as protective amulets. According to one account he roasted chicken with incantations and as they pulled pieces off the fowl the group chanted 'Thus we pull Buckra (the white man) to pieces.'[8] The revolutionary inspiration in the Old Testament, not without some traces of Reformed theology, was blended in Vesey's complex religious beliefs with traditional African religion, marking another break from the tailored Christianity in which he had been schooled.

There is no doubt that Vesey's theology left no room for forgiveness of enemies and oppressors. Certainly considerable plans were laid for the liberation of Charleston's black community and beyond. He called openly for a rebellion which involved killing a number of whites and African American 'collaborators', and some of these lived in fear of him. He would allow no questioning of tactics, let alone ideology, and it is fairly certain that he planned to lead an uprising in the not too distant future. But oppressive systems very easily fabricate resistance in order to tighten their control, and some have questioned whether the supposed plot was acted upon with slim or fabricated evidence to support it. Historians are divided over whether the planned rebellion of 1822 was a reality or a myth. One has described the evidence based on a 'handful of cooperative black witnesses who testified to what the court wanted them to say in order to save their own necks, when facing implication and execution'.[9]

At the end of May that year an enslaved man Peter Prioleau reported to his master that his friend William Paul had told him of a rumour of a great insurrection. Paul was arrested and questioned by the authorities. He admitted talking to Prioleau, but denied that rebellion

---

8. Higginson, 'Denmark Vesey', pp. 732, 733.
9. Michael Johnston, 'Denmark Vesey and his Co-Conspirators', *William and Mary Quarterly*, Vol. 58, n. 4 (2001), pp. 915-76. Johnston supported the assessment by Richard Wade, 'The Vesey Plot, a Reconsideration', *Journal of Southern History*, Vol. 30 (May 1964), pp. 143-61. Others who have disagreed are Robert Tinkler in his biography of James Hamilton in 2004 and James Spady in *William and Mary Quarterly*, Vol. 68 (Apr. 2011).

An extensive treatment of the subject and its debates is given in Ford, *Deliver us from Evil*, pp. 207-96.

had featured. However after incarceration for a week in the notorious workhouse and fearing that he would be executed, he confessed to the knowledge of a plot that would lead to a massacre of whites, led by a slave who 'carried a charm that rendered him invulnerable'.[10]

A key figure in the reaction of the authorities was an ambitious young lawyer, James Hamilton, recently elected Mayor of Charleston. With the testimony of the two slaves he organised a military style operation, arrested Vesey, 'Gullah' Jack, and scores of African Americans, enslaved and free. Sixty-seven men were convicted, after a closed trial at which the accused were denied any representation. Thirty-five were executed and 32 received other punishments. The official record of proceedings was edited by James Hamilton.

The procedure and verdict did not go unchallenged at the time. South Carolina's Governor Thomas Bennett, although condemning any rebellion, did not believe that there was sufficient evidence to warrant Hamilton's draconian action, and was horrified at the court procedure that violated even normal judicial practice. His brother-in-law William Johnston, a Supreme Court Judge, published in the *Charleston Courier* a piece titled 'The Melancholy Effect of Popular Sentiment'.

Hamilton and his supporters laid blame for incitement of the churches in Charleston and their support for the religious instruction of slaves along with the establishment of the Emmanuel AME Zion Church in the city. The church was burned down by a mob after the Vesey 'plot' became public, and Revd Morris Brown was imprisoned for many months without trial or evidence of any crime. All African American churches were banned by state law in 1834, and only after the Civil War was Emmanuel rebuilt.

In August 1822 *The Southern Intelligencer*, a Presbyterian controlled newspaper, whilst lauding the action taken by Hamilton, was severely critical of his attitude in his report, and reflected the outrage of ministers of various denominations. However none of this did anything to blunt Hamilton's electoral popularity, or diminish his support from the majority of whites. He served several terms in the

---

10. James Hamilton, *An Account of the Late Intended Insurrection Amongst a Portion of the Blacks of the City* (Charleston, 1822). This and another contemporary report are cited by Ford, *Deliver us from Evil*, pp. 207-08.

US House of Representatives and by the early 1830s was the Governor of South Carolina.[11]

Nat Turner (1800-1832) – Revolutionary Visionary

It was said that the year 1831 was a crucial one in the lives of African Americans. The event that did most to shape slavery in the South was the uprising in Southampton County, Virginia, the most *Confessions* which he dictated after his capture and before his trial.[12] He was born into slavery on a plantation extensive in American history to date. It was led by an enslaved person known as 'Nat' Turner.

Turner's early life and the accounts of this rebellion are mainly contained in the The Confessions owned by Benjamin Turner. 'Nat' claimed that even at the age of 4 he had extra-sensory powers, and said that his mother predicted he would be a prophet after he related in detail events that had happened before he was born. When at an early age he preached and led others in prayer, he felt the unbearable tension between the reality of his servitude, and the conviction of being called to a divine mission. Nat Turner had learnt to read and write, and devoured the scriptures, but in contrast to the analytical dissection of the Bible by Denmark Vesey, his own revolutionary inspiration came from mystic trances.

He liberated himself in 1821, but returned after a month, hungry, but convinced that the Spirit appeared to him claiming that he was 'directed to the things of this world', and that it was God's will for him to return to his master. Others around him who had also freed themselves told him that if he had any sense 'he would not serve any master in the world' but the conviction of the vision won out.[13]

Three years later, in the service of another master, Thomas Moore, he had a further vision in the fields in which he saw 'white spirits

---

11. Thomas Bennett, *The Melancholy Effect of Popular Excitement* (Privately printed in Charleston, 1822).
12. *The Confessions of Nat Turner, the Leader of the Late Insurrections in Southampton, Va as fully and voluntarily made to Thomas R. Gray, also an Authentic Account of the Whole Insurrection* (Published Thos Gray, Printed Lucas and Denver, 1831).
13. Ibid.

and black spirits engaged in battle, when the sun was darkened'. He described this, three years later, in 1828:

> I heard a loud noise in the heavens, and the Spirit instantly appeared to me and said the Serpent was loosened, and Christ had laid down the yoke he had borne for the sins of men, and that I should take it on and fight against the Serpent, for the time was fast approaching when the first should be last and the last first.

He believed that there would be a sign in the heavens. On the appearance of the sign, he said. he should prepare himself and slay his enemies with their own weapons. There was a sign (an eclipse of the sun in February 1831), but plans for the uprising were delayed because he was ill. When another sign appeared in August, 'it determined me', he said, 'to wait no longer'.

He gathered 70 followers, both enslaved and free, and went from house to house, freeing slaves and killing whites, including those in the household of his present 'owner' Joseph Travis, with whom he had been since 1830. Turner said in The Confessions that Travis was 'a kind master' from whom he had 'no cause' to complain of his treatment, but that did not diminish the certainty of his path. Turner was reported to have called on his followers to 'kill all whites' but he saw this as only an initial tactic to spread terror and alarm, and they spared many poor whites. Most of the killings and their methods are detailed in The Confessions.

In less than twelve hours after the start of the rising, militias from Virginia and South Carolina, assisted by Federal troops from a nearby garrison, overpowered the conspirators. White vigilantes, and some of the troops, defying the orders of the authorities, killed and maimed dozens of slaves and free persons of colour in revenge, and heads were placed on signposts on the roads to terrorise all who saw them.[14] Of those who were brought to court fifteen were hanged and seven transported out of Virginia. It has been estimated that approximately 160 African Americans lost their lives through attacks by mobs.

Nat Turner lived in the woods for several weeks. However a dog accompanied by two 'negroes' discovered him, and he had to change

---

14. Scott A. French, 'The Confessions of Nat Turner', *Encyclopedia Virginia* (Nov. 2008).

his hiding place. Shortly afterwards he surrendered to a local farmer, who threatened to shoot him. His only weapon was a small sword. He was brought to trial charged with 'making insurrection, and plotting to take away the lives of divers free white persons'. Although the *Confessions* were read and Nat Turner was reported not to add to them when questioned, he pled 'not guilty' to the charge, saying simply that he did not feel in any way guilty. When asked by Thomas Gray, who interviewed him in jail, if he regretted what he had done, his reply was 'Was not Christ crucified?' Nat Turner was hanged on 11 November.[15]

Thomas Gray came from a wealthy local family and had trained as a lawyer. He was not Nat Turner's counsel, but introduced the *Confessions*, which he claimed were a correct transcript of Turner's words to him when interviewed. Gray, who was in debt, sought to use the *Confessions* as a pamphlet, which was widely distributed. Although he failed to find a publisher at first in the South, and it was printed in Philadelphia, no less than 50,000 copies were sold both North and South. He claimed that it provided a means of public understanding of the motives behind the rebellion, and would replace 'a thousand idle, exaggerated, and mischievous reports' with one authoritative one.

To demonstrate authenticity he included a statement signed by six members of the court. This stated that the confessions were read to them, acknowledged by Turner 'to be full, free, and voluntary'. Gray added his own assessment of the *Confessions*. The words 'fanatic' and 'fanaticism' occur, and the killings are described as 'fiend-like barbarity'. He found the calmness with which the events are told 'chilling', yet he rejected any charges of ignorance or cowardice that had been suggested. He gave grudging respect to Turner's intelligence and knowledge and his acceptance of his fate.

Historians have been far less divided on the authenticity of Gray's narrative than that of the other lawyer Hamilton in the Vesey case. A novel by William Styron in 1967 was based on the *Confessions* and was widely acclaimed. However in an essay in 1993 linking Gray and Styron, Daniel Fabricant challenged this uncritical acceptance. He saw the *Confessions* as the work of a 'white racist' who was 'dedicated to the political, social, and economic interests of the Southern slavocracy' and said more about 'the victimisation of blacks that was carried out, under the guise of law and justice', than it revealed

---

15. Gray, *The Confessions*.

about Nat Turner.[16] All that was itself an authentic judgement on the system but it does not necessarily invalidate the account of the Turner rebellion.[17]

Both Demark Vesey and Nat Turner have been lauded as heroic figures in the African American community. The celebrated later abolitionist Frederick Douglass held Vesey in high regard and Henry 'Highland' Garnett, Presbyterian minister and revolutionary, described Turner in 1843 as one who will be remembered 'in future generations among the noble and the brave'. Only in recent years, and not without controversy and opposition from white groups, have lasting monuments been erected to both men. A house in Charleston, designated as Vesey's, became a National Monument in 1976 but it was 1994 before a statue was placed in a park in the northern suburbs of the city. Virginia has been even slower to recognise Nat Turner as a significant figure. In 2017 an Anti-Slavery Monument was constructed in Richmond, the state capital, and after fierce debate, centred on the white women and children killed in the rebellion (but not the unknown black women and men who suffered the revenge), the decision was taken to include Nat Turner.

Partly because of Governor Bennett's scepticism over the way in which the Vesey 'plot' was investigated and the trial that followed, South Carolina's official reaction was not as punitive to African Americans as it might have been. The executions and deportations at the time were severe, but they were orchestrated by Hamilton. There were adjustments to legislation tightening controls on free African Americans and skilled slaves who were able to travel about, but the application was left to local officials. As Ford observed, the oppression of free blacks and artisans in post-Vesey South Carolina lay in not knowing when and where the restrictions would be implemented.[18]

However more threatening was the reaction of many outside official quarters. In the spring of 1823 the South Carolina Association was formed, a prelude to the many white citizens councils throughout the

---

16. French, *The Confessions of Nat Turner*.
17. Ibid. William Styron, *The Confessions of Nat Turner* (New York: Random House, 1967); Daniel J. Fabricant, 'Thomas R. Gray and William Styron. 'Finally a Critical Look at the 1831 Confessions of Nat Turner', *American Journal of Legal History*, Vol. 37, no. 3 (July 1993), pp. 332-61.
18. Ford, *Deliver Us from Evil*, p. 281.

Rebellion and Reaction 49

South that were to terrorise African Americans over many years in the twentieth century. The founders of the Association included white planters, professionals, merchants and political leaders, with the aim of the 'better government' of enslaved and free people of colour. It enjoyed widespread popularity amongst whites, and claimed to be an unofficial police that would report any violations of the legislation. One of its prominent leaders was Whitemarsh Seabrook (1793-1855), later to be Governor of the State, who for several years kept up a torrent of criticism of what he saw as a 'lenient' attitude towards free African Americans.[19]

The Nat Turner rebellion led to further discussion throughout the Upper South on whether slavery was worthwhile, and in Virginia there were some attempts to stay any stringent measures to impose further controls. Even more surprising was a serious debate in the State Assembly over whether slavery was not worthwhile and might be abolished (and the state cleared of all African Americans).

What really frightened both parts of the South was a widely circulated pamphlet by an African American churchman David Walker (1796-1830), who had lived in Charleston during the Vesey 'plot', almost certainly had some contact with him, but moved to Boston in 1825 and became an anti-slavery writer. With assistance from the Grand African Freemasons Lodge Walker published in 1829 *An Appeal to the Colored Citizens of the World*. He died the next year from tuberculosis, but this pamphlet alone, which was distributed free and reprinted several times, has been rated as one of the influential document of nineteenth-century America, and a pioneer challenge to slavery from an African American.

Walker appealed to the free black community to mobilise and organise the destruction of slavery and of racism that proscribed their movements and activities. As a member of the African Methodist Episcopal Church community he argued that they should do more than offer prayer. Taking a text from Chronicles 20:15, 'be not afraid or dismayed', he urged action 'to gain freedom or natural right from under our cruel oppressors and murderers', but to plan 'when you see your ways clear, when that hour comes and you move'. He called for

---

19. Ibid., pp. 283-84, 304-30, . W. Seabrook, *A Concise View of the Critical Situation and Future Prospects of the Slave-holding States* (Charleston: A.E. Miller, 1825).

the rejection of any notion that the Bible sanctioned slavery, and urged whites to 'repent before God punished them for their wickedness'.

The pamphlet found its way through a network of distributors not just in the Upper but Lower South. In Louisiana which had a large proportion of free African Americans, legislation was pushed through preventing black seamen from remaining in the state's ports, as South Carolina and Georgia too. There was evidence that the pamphlet was taken on ships entering from the North. Ironically, in Mississippi, support for 'whitening' through the African Methodist Episcopal Church increased. All over the South white nerves were tightened over the prospect of the threat, not only to Church their livelihood but too their lives, and the Turner uprising seemed to justify those fears.

Walker declared his strong belief that education and a reorganised religious teaching was one of the main key towards liberation. 'The bare name of educating the colored people', he wrote, 'scares our cruel oppressors almost to death.'[20]

Preventative measures against literacy for both enslaved and free African Americans became a strong feature throughout the South following the Vesey and Turner activity – it was of course given greater impetus with the Walker pamphlet and the growth of abolition literature coming from the North – Garrison's *Liberator* followed shortly afterwards. However some legislation preventing literacy dated back to colonial times. At first it was only writing that was proscribed.

The 1740 Act in South Carolina stated that: 'All and every persons whatsoever, who shall hereafter teach or cause any slave or slaves to be taught to write, or shall use or employ any slave as a scribe … every person or persons shall for every such offence, forfeit the sum of one hundred pounds.' However in the Act it also stated that 'the allowing of slaves to read' would be 'attended with many inconveniences'. By 1800 the law had been tightened up, inflicting 20 lashes on 'any slave found in an assembly convened for the purpose of "mental instruction"', even in the presence of a white person. Georgia

---

20. David Walker, *Walkers Appeal, in Four Articles, Together with a Preamble , to the Colored Citizens of the World, but in Particular, and very expressedly to those of the United States of America, written in Boston, State of Massachusetts, September 28th 1829*. Library of Congress.

followed suit in 1759 but it was well into the next century before the legal bans on reading took place.

Virginia in 1819 prohibited slaves and 'free negroes' from 'mixing' in assemblies but it was only after the Turner uprising that any education was forbidden. In a personal testimony William Allan recalled that the Virginia Assembly: 'Immediately, as an act of retaliation or vengeance, abolished every colored school within their borders and having dispersed the pupils, ordered the teachers to leave the State forthwith and never more to return.'[21] With strange irony that same Assembly debated seriously whether to abolish slavery.

By this time the Lower South had consistently passed legislation criminalising literacy. South Carolina and Georgia led the way and most other states followed after 1831. The Congressman James Henry Hammond from South Carolina argued that it was madness for anyone to allow slaves to learn reading, since they could then get access to 'incendiary literature'. Bizarrely, as a Protestant, he argued that the Catholic Church had had to deny the scriptures to the ignorant and impressionable in Europe; William Harper, Speaker of the State House of Representatives and son of a Methodist missionary, supported him in declaring 'the slave receives such instructions as qualifies him for his particular station'.[22]

In 1835 Edmund Bellinger, a prominent planter and public figure in South Carolina, said: 'The negro is from his intellectual and moral organisation incapable of being civilised or enjoying freedom; utterly incompetent to become a citizen of a civilised community.' If blacks were free, he added, they would 'corrupt the principles of one half of our population and drag them down – down to their own depraved, degraded and disgusting condition'.

He ended this crude racist analysis by setting it in the context of world history where he affirmed that no country could contain 'free races of men too distinct to amalgamate'. It would, he grandly proclaimed, lead to extermination of one or the other.[23]

---

21. W. Allan, *A short Personal Narrative* (Dublin: sold by the author, 1860), p. 6.
22. Genovese, *Roll, Jordan, Roll*, pp. 561-62.
23. Edmund Bellinger, *A Speech on the Subject of Slavery: Delivered 7 September 1835 at a Public Meeting of the Citizens of Barnwell District, South Carolina* (Charleston: D. Dowling, 1835), cited in Ford, *Deliver us from Evil*, pp. 509-10.

Bellinger was not so unrepresentative in his views. This demonstrates the difficulties faced by leading white churchmen in South Carolina and Georgia who sought ways of bringing the Christian Gospel to free and enslaved African Americans, and to help them to develop their own style of Christianity. This was an uphill task, increasingly so as the country moved closer to Civil War, when any middle ground on slavery was no longer accepted as tenable.

Chapter 5

Paternalism and Colonialism

They are a class separated from ourselves by their color, their position in society, their relation to our families, their national origin, and their moral, intellectual, and physical condition. Nowhere are the poor so closely and intimately connected with the higher classes than are our poor with us. They belong to us. We also belong to them.... they are our poor, our poor brethren; children of our God and Father, dear to our Savior.
—Revd John Adger, Second Presbyterian Church, Charleston, May 1847

Africa, the land of our fathers, although surrounded with clouds of darkness, seems to me to be extending her arms towards us as her only hope of relief, and calling on us loudly for help – saying 'I struggle for light and liberty, and call upon you by the names of your ancestors, to come to my help and your rightful possession.'
—Charles Henry, Church Leader, Charleston, December 1830

What to Do about Slavery?

One chapter in a major study of the old South is headed 'Owning Slaves, Disowning Slavery'.[1] We have already seen this awkward disjunction through the eyes of some prominent Presbyterians in the

---
1. Lacy K. Ford, *Deliver us from Evil*.

early days of the new republic, when the public fight for political and religious liberty was combined, sometimes with little self-awareness, with the irony of holding human beings in bondage. At an early stage some Southerners termed this 'a stern necessity', occasioned by economics. Kenneth Stampp argued that most Southerners struggled with guilt, but were too deeply involved in probable material loss to consider emancipation. Nonetheless he maintained that they 'knew that slavery betrayed the American tradition of individual liberty and natural rights and that the attack (on slavery by abolitionists) was in the main valid'. He went on to argue that it was because of this uncertainty that many 'slave-owners' lacked the full commitment to the Southern cause that might have made the result of the war different.[2] Others disagreed, including, at first, the formidable chronicler of the world that slaves made, Eugene Genovese, but more recently he argued that the Protestant influence in the South and the difficulty of reconciling the Bible with slavery led to much underlying guilt.[3]

Attitudes towards slavery were far from uniform throughout the South, nor were they static in the years leading up to the Civil War. During the Revolutionary War many enslaved people managed to liberate themselves either by joining the British forces, or by finding their way to Canada. The ever present threat of rebellion made many in the Upper South (the Border States plus Tennessee and North Carolina) feel that, if slavery could be diminished, these difficulties would be eased. It was not that the abolitionist movement took hold, but there was an attractiveness to what became seen as a 'whitening' of these states, getting rid of as many enslaved people and indeed free blacks as possible. Nowadays we would speak of 'ethnic cleansing'.

They saw two ways of making this possible. By the beginning of the nineteenth century the tobacco sales and production in states such as Virginia had declined, as had the urgent need for intensive labour. On

---

2. Kenneth Stampp, *The Imperilled Union: Essays on the Background of the Civil War* (New York: Oxford University Press, 1980), p. 263. Kimberley Kellison, 'Towards Humanitarian Ends? Protestants and Slave Reform in South Carolina 1830-1865', *South Carolina Historical Magazine*, Vol. 103 (July 2002).
3. Eugene Genovese, *A Consuming Fire: The Fall of the Confederacy in the Mind of the White Christian South* (Athens, GA: University of Georgia Press, 1998), pp. 32-33, 22. Genovese is cited by Kellison, 'Towards Humanitarian Ends?' pp. n210-25.

the other hand the cotton boom in the South required an increasing number of workers on plantations in Georgia, South Carolina and Mississippi. In 1808 the external slave trade was banned by law in the United States. Ports such as Charleston, which had imported thousands of Africans each year, could not, officially at least, continue to do so. There was therefore a ready market for sales of human beings from the Upper to the Lower South. Many 'slave-owners' in the Upper South found this an attractive way of easing their burden, enabling them to diversify economically, and even perhaps quieten their consciences.

Secondly, schemes to colonise Africa attracted quite a few whites. African Americans could be settled in the continent and their numbers in the United States would be diminished. Although such a scheme of American colonisation, when first proposed, drew some considerable support from legislators and key citizens in some Northern states, as well as those in the Upper South, it was far more problematical in the Lower South, and especially amongst many leading African Americans. It attracted however some whites and blacks who were fired with evangelical zeal to spread the Gospel in Africa, and to establish Christian communities there.

'Whitening', or diminishing the number of African Americans, was not an option in the states of the Lower South. The cotton boom and the cultivation of rice in the swamplands needed an intense form of labour that existed by coercion and control through ownership and total domination. In this new republic, where white men, if not women, took pride in being beholden to none for 'life, liberty, and the pursuit of happiness', it was seen as essential for continuing prosperity to have others, indelibly marked by the visibly obvious, to give unquestioning lifetime service. That service could be domestic, where the unfree catered for every domestic whim or, for the majority, heavy and unremitting work in the production of wealth.

There were of course disadvantages to this system. If guilt over slavery was felt by some 'slave-owners', far more were gripped with fear – fear of the unpredictable, of rebellion and of not being able to force submission in all situations. Many felt more secure in assessing the behaviour of their dogs than the enslaved human beings under their control. Of course there were many variations of approach, as there always are in others who hold authority in institutions, but the fear factor on both sides was very common, and was reflected in the reaction to the upheavals in Charleston in 1822 and Virginia in 1831.

The New Doctrine of 'Paternalism'

A movement to cope with the complexity of slavery was associated in the late eighteenth century with a theoretical need to treat enslaved people more as human beings than as simply property. It was termed 'paternalism' and a few claimed that this 'humanitarianism' owed something to the intellectual influence of the Scottish Enlightenment, but also to the moral message from the religious revival movement known as the Great Awakening.[4] Of course it was far from universally embraced by plantation owners in the South, as so many reports of the reality of life there testify. But it was to be eagerly seized on by many leading churchmen, and was a large part of the enthusiasm to bring the Gospel to those on the plantations.

Lacey K. Ford outlined the ideological principles of paternalism in four propositions. First, while acknowledging their supposed inferiority and 'limited potential', it was argued that those who were enslaved must be recognised as human beings and not as beasts or objects. Secondly, the ordering of an enslaved population should be modelled on the way in which male heads of families were expected to govern their own households – wives and children. This should be fair but firm, and demonstrate a balance of affection and discipline. It was claimed that it would lead to more efficient labour and help to subdue any unrest.

Thirdly a demand of stewardship towards the captives should be required from the masters. Those who advocated it overwhelmingly came from a Christian tradition, and churchmen were required to take it up. To this was added the responsibility of Christian teaching and encouragement in the faith. For 'masters' it was all part of the obligation to strive for a society that embraced these ideals, and to influence white neighbours to act accordingly.[5]

In his major survey of the world of the enslaved Genovese claimed that

> A paternalism accepted by both masters and slaves – but with radically different interpretations – afforded a fragile

---

4. Joyce E. Chaplin, "Slavery and the Principle of Humanity: A Modern Idea in the Early Lower South', *Journal of Social History* Vol. 24 Dec. 1990 pp. 229-315.
5. Ford, *Deliver us from Evil*, p. 145.

> bridge across the intolerable contradictions inherent in a society based on racism, slavery, and class exploitation that had to depend on the willing reproduction and productivity of its victims. For the 'slave-owners' paternalism represented an attempt to overcome the fundamental contradiction in slavery: the impossibility of the slave ever becoming the things they were supposed to be. Paternalism defined the involuntary labor of the slaves as a legitimate return to their masters for protection and direction.[6]

Yet he argued that paternalism weakened resistance and solidarity with other enslaved people. It encouraged identification with specific families, and fragmented the possibility of group, race and class identity. It may have mitigated the effects of slavery where it was followed, but by helping to build an ordered society with tight social relationships in its individual parts, it helped to blunt the possibility of rebellion and self-liberation for the enslaved.[7]

Although appeals to self-interested security and morality were used to persuade 'slave-owners' to adopt a paternalistic approach and mitigate the harshness of slavery, a further and powerful one was that of economics and profitability. Many pamphlets and manuals for running slave plantations argued, as did many correspondents, that humane treatment of slaves, proper provisions and working conditions, would result in more productivity and a greater profit margin.

The paternalist vision harked back to many similar schemes of management of people in history, not least in the lands from which settlers in the South, or their more recent ancestors, had come. The feudal system in Europe assumed a responsibility of landowners for the welfare of their tenants, who in turn had the obligation of service. It may not have been an absolute system of ownership, although in some cases it was near enough. The clan system in Scotland had these elements, although after the defeat of the Jacobite rising in 1745, which took many to the Americas, its mutuality finally died a death.

It was the ordered society that many 'slave-owners' sought, and certainly those who controlled the governance of the South at this time looked to a society where all knew their places, and these were

---

6. Genovese, *Roll, Jordan, Roll*, p. 5.
7. Ibid., pp. 5, 6.

recognised as immutable conditions for civilisation. There grew up a concept of the Southern 'way of life', which was often more noticeable in its violation than observance, but proved, as the defences of slavery later showed, to be a powerful and comforting myth. Paternalism fitted neatly into this, giving a moral basis for what, it would have hoped, would build a wall against any challenge to the system.

Tools of Evangelism

The Reformed tradition with its roots in Calvin's Geneva developed the doctrine of predestination, the idea that there were those who were immutably chosen of God. Its roots of course were one part of the Exodus story in the Old Testament that told of God's special favour towards the Israelites, as they conquered other lands and dominated (or slaughtered) the inhabitants. This was the driving force for those mid-eighteenth-century Dutch settlers in South Africa, and its legacy lasted in some form for two and a half centuries, more recently under the doctrine of Apartheid. Needless to say, the other half of the story, the liberation from slavery in Egypt, was conveniently adapted on pseudo-racial lines.

When Rev John Adger (1810-99) from one of Charleston's wealthiest families, returned from Presbyterian mission work in Armenia in 1847, he sought the endorsement of the Second Presbyterian Church in the city to act as a missionary to the city's African American population, both enslaved and free. In the extract from his sermon at the start of this chapter, the theological argument for paternalism is clearly seen. His text was 'The poor have the gospel preached unto them.' It was a message that would not automatically fall on sympathetic ears, since there was nervousness very much around about the prospect of any interference with the status quo, particularly since memories were still fresh of the claimed plot to enflame the city in a slave rebellion from a quarter of a century beforehand.[8] The sermon was a measured statement that did not mention the word 'slaves', or 'servants', as Southern whites preferred to describe their 'property', which attempted to sanitise the institution. Adger did refer to 'belonging' to each other, and that held a message of benevolence and order, with each one in their allotted place.

---

8. Cited in Clarke, *Our Southern Zion*, p. 190.

Paternalism and Colonialism

Adger continued with a vision of enslaved and free being bound together in a settled domestic order throughout life. 'Our mothers confine us when infants to their arms', he said, 'and sometimes to the milk of their breasts' and continued the picture:

> Their children are, to some extent, unavoidably, the playmates of our childhood – grow up with us under the same roof – sometimes pass through all the changes of life with us, and then they either stand weeping by our bedsides – or else we drop a tributary tear by theirs, when death comes to close the long connection and to separate the good master and his good servant.[9]

There may have been some enslaved people who stood weeping by the bedside of their masters. Those who laboured in the fields were unlikely to be entering on a deathbed, and domestic servants were very much in the minority. Even less likely would there be many 'masters' found weeping by a dying man or woman in the slave quarters. But although it painted a picture of ordered domestic bliss and mutuality, which in later years of post-war segregation and oppression was held up to question, yet in a meeting such as this it undergirded a comfortable assumption to an all-white audience that the institution allowed every opportunity for creating a Godly society, enabling the oppression of slavery to be swept under the carpet of benevolent domination, and claimed to be beneficial to both sides of the yawning divide.

The church may have colluded with this system, but within it considerable attempts were made to advance the Christian education envisaged by the Reformers in Scotland, and of course a direct result of the Great Commission given by Jesus in Matthew's gospel to bring the good news to all peoples.[10] In the spring of 1845 a gathering took place in including many wealthy planters. Among them was Robert Barnham Rhett, a firebrand defender of Southern interests, later to be in the Senate. Another was Thomas Drayton Grimke, whose sisters Emile and Sarah were strong abolitionists and advocates of women's rights in Philadelphia, where they now lived. For three days they discussed the issues of religious instruction to enslaved and free

---

9. Ibid.
10. Matthew 28:19-20.

blacks. What would be the most effective way of evangelisation? Was it safe to allow blacks to worship in their own churches, and in their own way? What would the effect be on discipline and order? Would it encourage rebellious thoughts?[11]

The meeting asked a Committee to draw up a paper titled *An Address to the Public*, that might be used to convince the white population of the city to accept religious instruction for black people. It started with the doctrine of Providence which, not unlike predestination, saw the ordaining by God of the status quo. Through the Providence of God, it stated, blacks had been brought from Africa (clearly a heathen continent where they were lost for eternity) and had been placed in the hands of whites 'by divine revelation'. It was therefore the sacred responsibility laid on whites to impart the blessings of Christianity to those under their care and control.[12]

Religious instruction was therefore co-opted as a vital element in the management and control of enslaved people. As Erskine Clarke observed 'religious and social forces were closely interwoven. There was a reciprocal relationship between the two.' This, for him, meant that all religious instruction was paternalistic. It put an emphasis on the personal responsibility of the masters and the enslaved rather than concentrating on the social structures, and in that way simply enshrined the present. It was a Middle Way to 'treat their black slaves as spiritual brothers and sisters without seeking to free them from their cruel bondage'.[13]

It was a different matter to persuade the white citizens of Charleston to permit black ministries or black churches. The accounts of many enslaved people witness to the tight control that was a strong feature of their experience of church – white preachers naturally in the places that they attended with the 'master's' family, but almost always their own worship was only permitted if supervised by whites.

In cities such as Charleston or Savannah in Georgia, the economic demands were more varied, and skilled bondsmen (though rarely

---

11. *On the Religious Instruction of Negroes, together with the Report of the Committee and the Address to the Public* (Charleston: B. Jenkins, 1845), p. 15. Cited by Erskine Clarke, *Wrestlin' Jacob: A Portrait of Religion in the Old South of religion in the old South* (Atlanta, GA: John Knox Press, 1979, pp. 102-07.
12. *On the Religious Instruction of Negroes* p. XX.
13. Erskine Clark, Wrestlin' Jacob: A Portrait of Religion in the Old South (Atlanta, Ga: John Knox Press, 1979).

bondswomen) were hired out to local businesses by their owners. As in the Upper South, there were more 'free blacks' in those cities and some limited mobility was far more the norm than in the rural areas. Emmanuel African Episcopal Church had not been popular with Charleston whites for long before the Vesey 'rebellion'. In 1818 140 members had been arrested and eight leaders given fines and lashes, for breaking city ordinances designed to limit black religious activity. City officials raided the church in 1820 and 1821. Tragically nearly two centuries later June a young white supremist, Dylan Roof, entered that same church on 17 June 2015 and shot and killed nine members at a Bible Study Group.[14]

A Church for Blacks Run by Whites

John Adger sought in the 1840s to establish a Presbyterian church that would give African Americans a spiritual home and more independence for worship. Given the suspicion in white circles of any independent African American worship, slave or free, it was a bold vision shared with Episcopalians that two churches be erected in Charleston. Calvary Episcopal Church and Anson Street Presbyterian Church were completed in 1850, once again after considerable difficulty. A mob threated to tear down the partly built Calvary, and only after expensive negotiations and the assurance that there would be white control was the project completed.

Neither church seemed to fulfil its purpose at the start. Adger served as pastor for two years at Anson Street which had room for 600 worshippers. Initially it attracted few African Americans, as did Calvary. But by the mid-1850s the Presbytery had allowed Anson Street Church to be independent of Second Presbyterian, and under a dynamic minister it was renamed Zion by its now considerable number of African American members. Some significant changes took place. In the reverse of the usual pattern, black members sat downstairs and whites upstairs, African American leaders were given scope for pastoral and administrative work, and surnames were used on the church roll – a departure from the ways that free blacks as well as enslaved people were normally simply denoted by their first names.[15] Yet ultimate control in the church resided in the hands of whites. Real partnership was a vision yet to be fully realised in twenty-first-century

---

14. CNN News, 17 June 2015.
15. Clarke, *Our Southern Zion*, pp. 190-97.

America, but certainly never remotely attempted in that part of the experiment known as paternalism.

Colonisation or Ethnic Cleansing?

The Society for the Colonisation of Free People of Color, or as it became known, the American Colonisation Society (ACS), was founded in Washington in December 1816 by Revd Robert Finley (1772-1817), a Presbyterian minister and President of the University of Georgia. Its objects, defined by him, 'to colonize (with their consent) the free people of color residing in our country, in Africa, or such other place as Congress may deem most expedient'.[16] There was from the beginning the assumption that free blacks, let alone those enslaved, were 'residents' of America rather than citizens, and if a return to Africa was not 'expedient', then somewhere else would do. It was a none too hidden expression of convenient ethnic cleansing.

At the start there was enthusiasm for the ACS from leading figures in the Upper South, including the wealthy planter and politician Henry Clay (1817-52) in Kentucky and former US Presidents, Thomas Jefferson and James Madison, all of whom of course were 'slave-owners'. Branches were set up throughout the United States, and even far into the Lower South. But soon colonisation began to divide the South further. The Lower South States saw, with some justification, that this might encourage their bondsmen and women to seek a way of throwing off the shackles, and from the start there was considerable resistance.

In 1819 Congress passed a Slave Trade Act which considerably tightened up the legislation of a decade previously, and President James Munro granted $100,000 to the Society in order to establish a colony on the West African coast to be known as Liberia. The timing was not accidental. The grant was applied for under the justification of wishing to 'dispose of recaptured Africans' under the new Act, with them returned to Africa rather than being sold. In 1820 the first ship sailed for the coast, with three white agents from the Society and 88 African Americans. Four years later the centre of the settlement was named Monrovia, in honour of the one who had funded them.[17]

---

16. Ford,.*Deliver us from Evil*, p. 71.
17. Ibid., p. 72.

Was colonisation an opportunity for the enslaved to find freedom, or for those supposedly 'free' blacks to find dignity in a new continent? Was it a covert attempt to hasten emancipation and weaken the institution of slavery? Was it simply a crude attempt at ethnic cleansing to reduce the number of black Americans in the country? Was it an opportunity to pioneer missionary work, and bring the Gospel (and civilisation) to a supposed 'dark' continent?

All these elements were advanced by advocates or opponents of colonisation. Initially it found a welcome amongst many in the states of the Upper South, who saw no future for free blacks in America and embraced the racial attitude of 'whitening'. It accepted that there was no prospect of a society where black and white could freely coexist. Ironically, nearly a century later, that was the conviction of some prominent African Americans who advocated a move to Africa.[18]

The movement has been described as a 'surrogate' for anti-slavery, where abolitionist sentiment was counterproductive, if not dangerous. The work of the ACS initially hoped to persuade 'slave-owners' who harboured some doubts, to have a way out towards emancipation without increasing the number of free blacks. Maryland, who had many such, were enthusiastic, as were other parts of the Upper South, including North Carolina and Tennessee.[19]

That was short-lived, and was never rooted in the Lower South. However the appeal of the ACS in 1824 for state endorsement of Federal funds to further the scheme, was supported by not just by a number of Northern states but by Delaware and Kentucky, which gave support, declaring that 'no jealousies ought to exist, on the part of this or other slave-holding States' over the issue.[20] Yet in the Lower South opposition was mobilised, and there was no doubt that many powerful voices saw it as an attempt to abolish an institution on which not just their economy, but their society, depended.

William Lloyd Garrison, as a young reporter and before becoming a leading abolitionist and editor of *The Liberator* in 1830, had been an early supporter of the ACS. But in 1832 he published a pamphlet

---

18. The celebrated author, academic and activist, W.E.B. Du Bois (1868-1963) who spent his last days in Ghana was and advocate for the Back to Africa movement in the mid-twentieth century.
19. David Brion Davis, *The Problem of Slavery in the Age of Revolution 1770-1823* (Ithaca, NY: Cornell University Press, 1973), pp. 199, 200.
20. Ford, *Deliver us from Evil,* p. 303.

that contained his reasons for his strong opposition. After contending that men of wealth and status were its most fervent supporters, and that the powerful 'Weapon' of the press had been 'seduced, and that populist prejudice had been used' he continued: 'I am constrained to declare with the utmost sincerity that I look on the colonisation schemes as inadequate in its design, injurious in its operation, and contrary to sound principle, and the more scrupulously I examine its pretensions, the stronger is my conviction of its sinfulness.'[21]

There were some strange sources of support for colonisation. One Virginia planter offered freedom to fourteen enslaved persons, if they would agree to go to Liberia at the expense of the ACS. All but one agreed. The Society's journal the *African Repository* in 1827 reported that a South Carolinian had offered to free 25 enslaved men and women and their children, who were 'willing and even anxious' to go to Africa. In 1836 Isaac Ross of Prospect Hill, Mississippi, in his will freed nearly 123 enslaved people, with the proviso that they should go to Liberia for twelve years. There followed local white hostility, and vigilante groups and lynchings prevented this. In the end, thirteen years later, a number boarded the *Laura* in New Orleans in January 1849 and set sail.[22]

Very few black figures supported the ACS but some, alongside some white clergy, saw it as a vehicle for enabling what had been the vision of Robert Finlay. Early in the Society's life the First Baptist Church in Richmond, Virginia, financed and appointed Lott Carey, a free man, as the first black missionary to Africa under the auspices of the ACS. He lived in Liberia until his death in an accident in 1828, having become Acting Governor of the colony for two years. As Lawrence Jones pointed out, his farewell sermon before departure from Virginia reveals considerable indoctrination in attitudes to Africa:

> I am about to leave you and expect to see your faces no more. I long to preach to the poor Africans the way of life

---

21. William Lloyd Garrison, *Thoughts on African Colonialization* (Boston, 1832), introduction. Garrison (1805-79) would be known as one of the leading white abolitionists in America. He travelled to Scotland in 1846 where he addressed meetings on slavery.

22. Stampp, *The Peculiar Institution*, p. 94; Ford, *Deliver us from Evil*, p. 314; Alan Huffman, *Mississippi in Africa* (New York: Gotham Books, 2005).

and salvation. I don't know what may befall me, whether I may find a grave in the ocean, or among the strange savage men, or more savage wild beasts, on the coast of Africa,[23]

When a meeting took place of 'free people of color' in Charleston on 6 December 1830 the topic for discussion was whether to support emigration to Liberia or not. Charles Henry was elected Secretary. He made a strong appeal for emigration, not merely as settlers, but missionaries. He argued, in the extract at the beginning of this chapter, that Africa was calling for the light of the Gospel and continued in the same appeal:

> Tarry not, but come over and dispel the darkness of your benighted land. Come and inspire us by your example, with sentiments of virtue and with a love of the duties taught by the meek and lowly Jesus. Come and enforce the empire of reason, truth, and Christianity over our benighted minds.

A large number from that meeting were to set sail for Liberia in 1832. Charles Henry and his family died of fever within a few months, as did many of those who came from Charleston at that time.

Some of those black Charlestonian settlers encountered Leighton and Jane Wilson, who arrived in Liberia in 1834 as Presbyterian missionaries. Leighton had been brought up in rural South Carolina and Jane in Savannah, Georgia. Both had inherited enslaved men and women, and had started to make arrangements for their freedom before going to Africa. Over the seventeen years there, until ill health determined their return, they founded schools, translated the Bible into local languages and exhibited some of the best qualities of early nineteenth-century missionaries. Deeply concerned about the persistence of slavery in their native land, they also saw the tensions between colonists, black and white in Liberia and indigenous Africans, and ironically found themselves at odds with African American officials in the colony who resented missionary interference into the trade established with visiting slave ships.[24]

---

23. Jones, *African Americans and the Churches*, pp. 145, 146.
24. Erskine Clarke,*By the Rivers of Water- A Nineteenth Century Atlantic Odyssey*(New York: Basic Books 2013), pp. 92, 146, 214.

Liberia was an American Colony from 1821 until independence in 1848. The colony took a terrible death toll. Of the 4,571 who emigrated between 1820 and 1843 only 1,819 survived.

The foundations of both the United States and Liberia involved compromise, negotiation, exclusion and many other issues as both coped with the ideals of freedom in the midst of the African and the international slave trade. The tensions between settlers and the indigenous African population were never resolved, and the tragic results of this were seen until well into this century.

Perhaps Lyman Beecher (1775-1863), Presbyterian minister, educator, and father of Harriet Beecher Stowe, made an honest assessment of colonisation when he said in 1834: 'It is not necessary that the Colonization Society should be, or claim to be, an adequate remedy for slavery. Her great and primary object, is the emancipation of Africa, while she anticipated as an incidental result, the emancipation of the colored race at home.'[25]

As with paternalism, colonisation was a forlorn attempt to make palatable a system that it would take a war to destroy.

---

25. *Cincinnati Journal*, 13 Jun 1834.

Chapter 6

Religious Education and Slaveholding

Do not the majority of our citizens who make this objection, consider slavery sanctioned by the Bible? Why then do they hesitate to have the Bible, the whole Bible, and nothing but the Bible preached to their servants?
—Revd Charles C. Jones, Speech to Synod of Georgia and South Carolina, 3 December 1831

Our design in giving them the Gospel, is not to civilise them, not to change their social condition – nor to exalt them into citizens of freemen – it is to save them.
—Revd James Henley Thornwell, 'Slavery and the Religious Instruction of the Colored People', *Southern Presbyterian Review* (July 1850)

Months after the Nat Turner uprising, a young Presbyterian minister spoke to a deliverance which he proposed to the Presbyterian Synod of Georgia and South Carolina meeting in Charleston. It stressed the urgency of evangelism of enslaved people. In a passionate address he challenged the Presbyterian church in the deep South not to betray the Gospel injunction for the sake of other motives:

> Shall thousands and even millions of immortal minds be sacrificed at the throne of cupidity? What ought to prevail,

for the good of mankind, – for the glory of our country, for the prosperity of the cause of God – Principle or Interest? Right or Wrong? Let the enlightened conscience of the philanthropist, of the patriot, and of the Christian, return the answer.[1]

The Synod accepted the responsibility for religious education for those enslaved. It was a bold move, since most whites (and that meant the great majority of members of Presbyterian churches) were seeking ways of limiting any opportunities for all people 'of color' in their midst to safeguard their security. Perhaps with that in mind, the Synod felt that it had to attach the words of caution to the deliverance:

> The Synod deeply sympathise with the people of South Carolina and Georgia in their present feeling with regard to our coloured population. They and many of them, interested in this species of a property and feel themselves bound to do anything in their power to communicate such religious instruction as is in perfect correspondence with the civil institutions of our country.[2]

Even the recognition of slavery as ownership of 'property' and one of the central 'civil institutions of our country' would not calm the fervour of the Hammonds, the Harpers and the Bellinger's. But a letter in the *Charleston Observer* a few months later, making reference to the recent painful 'excitement' throughout the country, asked where should a remedy come from that would 'extinguish the flame of discontent'. The correspondent observed that something was needed to: 'Render the negro more happy and contented in existing circumstances. And what is so eminently calculated to effect this, as the principles of the Christian religion, deeply and graciously impressed on his heart.'[3]

---

1. Erskine Clark, *Dwelling Place: A Plantation Epic* (New Haven :Yale University Press, 2005) pp.107-8, Minutes of the Synod of South Carolina and Georgia, 3 Dec. 1831. Presbyterian Historical Foundation, Montrest, NC.
2. Ibid.
3. *Charleston Observer,* 4 Feb. 1832.

Charles Colcock Jones (1804-1863) – Slave-Owner and Missionary

That last sentiment would have well expressed the mission of the mover of the Synod's deliverance, Revd Charles Colcock Jones. Jones was a rare example of an actively involved plantation owner, missionary and preacher, scholar and teacher rolled into one. Erskine Clarke, who traces the history of plantation life and the Jones family of south coastal Georgia, describes him as 'a leading advocate for the reform of slavery in an attempt to make the system more humane'.[4]

Jones was born on the ironically named Liberty Hall plantation in south-east Georgia, and trained for the Presbyterian ministry in Andover Newton Seminary in Massachusetts and Princeton. At Andover he developed a strong revulsion to slavery, describing it in a letter to Mary his fiancée in Georgia as 'a violation of all the laws of God, at once a complete annihilation of justice' and 'an inhuman use of power'. It was 'a great evil'. Andover was very much influenced by the New England 'awakening' with its new religious spirit and its practical outcome on moral issues. It challenged the young Georgian, and during his time there and a year at Princeton, he wrestled with his conscience. For a short while he was tempted to support colonisation, and more drastically he considered emancipation of the many slaves he now owned.

Princeton strangely may have been the catalyst for the difficult roles of being not only a minister, but a missionary to the enslaved whilst 'owning' and managing them. In earlier days Princetonians such as Witherspoon and Ramsay had recognised the structural evil of slavery but accommodated themselves to it in the short term. Jones in another letter to Mary describes the Calvinist theology of Princeton as an acceptance of everything as from the grace of God, even repentance, and he affirmed that God would destroy evil in his own time.[5] He rejected that literal aspect of predestination and held to the

---

4. Erskine Clarke's biographical history of the Jones family and their enslaved families, the plantation, and mission of Charles Colcock Jones was described by David Brion Davis as 'one of the best and most important studies of American slavery I have ever read'. Jones' concern for religious education is described in this and the earlier study, *Wrestlin Jacob*.
5. Clarke, *Dwelling Place*, p. 87.

responsibility to repent of evil, but it may have given him a gateway towards the acceptance of God's time for bringing slavery to an end and therefore in the meantime working within it.

In 1830 Jones he returned to rural Georgia, but shortly afterwards served as Minister of the First Presbyterian Church in the city of Savannah. By this time he had become the owner of three large plantations through gifts from relatives and his marriage. Not only did he throw himself into a plan for evangelism on his own land, but he was determined to promote this amongst his fellow farmers. Soon after his return to the South, he called a meeting of 29 planters, among them many wealthy families in the area, and shared with them his vision. He preached to them on the text 'Go ye into all the world and preach the Gospel to every creature.' In it he strongly pressed the obligations to give Christian education to their 'servants'. But he was careful to avoid any mention of slavery as 'sin', let alone hint at eventual emancipation. He appealed to their prejudices by a somewhat crude tirade on the supposed moral failures of enslaved people on their plantations – 'they lie, steal, blaspheme, are slothful, deceivers'. He stated that many enslaved men and women on the plantations didn't go to church, could not tell who Jesus was and had no idea of the Ten Commandments.

The implication was that, if this was rectified, enslaved people would be better and more reliable workers and that this would be of great benefit to those who owned them. Not all were convinced, but enough were persuaded to form the Liberty County Association for the Religious Instruction of Negroes. Jones offered to meet expenses out of his now considerable financial resources, and offered his services as a missionary without payment for seven years.[6] He gave a detailed annual report to the Association every January.

In effect Charles Jones served in this capacity as a missionary for fifteen years, whilst at the same time helping to launch the new Presbyterian Theological Seminary in Columbia and teaching for a brief time as Professor of Church History there. In his ministry in Savannah he reached out to the African American community, and was invited to preach in several of their gatherings. At the same time he sought, through example on his own plantations, to show that slavery could be more humane, He not only preached to those who worked for

---

6. Clarke, *Wrestlin' Jacob*, pp. 24-28; *Dwelling Place*, pp. 99-106.

him, but he visited them regularly as a pastor, and attempted to serve them as well as to control them.

The document which best encapsulates Jones' philosophy is his *Catechism of Scripture, Doctrine and Practice for Families and Sabbath Schools designed also for the Oral Instruction of Coloured Persons*. This was a collection which he devised when teaching at Columbia Seminary, and it was published in 1835. The last part of the title kept it within the laws of literacy, which Jones and some of his white ministerial colleagues found so inhibiting. In addition to doctrine it included hymns, prayers, commandments and a table of Questions and Answers on the duties of husbands and wives, parents and children, masters and servants.

The *Catechism* makes clear a Christian responsibility for the 'religious instruction of negroes'. With what seems to modern eyes us a descent into racist paternalism, Jones wrote: 'Their depravity, their spiritual ignorance, and their destitution are amazingly and awfully great. They cry out for instruction to the wise and good, in all the length and breadth of the land.' But it does at least recognise that, where instruction is attempted, more than a few simple questions and answers are required. This minimalist approach for Jones was superficial. 'On the contrary', he wrote, 'we should aim to carry the people of our care through a regular and plain system of Scripture doctrine and practice and thus put them in full possession of the plan of salvation.'[7]

Interestingly he put the Duties of Masters first. He quoted scripture against abusing, cruelly punishing or overworking servants, and laid the responsibility on masters to provide 'comfortable houses, comfortable clothing, wholesome and abundant food', laying himself open to any to check whether Montevideo, Maybank and Arcadia, his own plantations provided all of these things. 'What command has God given to masters?' is one of the questions and the answer is given 'Masters give unto your servants that which is just and equal: knowing that ye also have a master in Heaven.'[8] Jones made it clear that the 'master' is bound to 'instruct servants in a knowledge of the

---

7. Charles C. Jones, *A Catechism of Scripture: Doctrine and Practice for Families and Sabbath Schools, also designed for the Oral Instruction of Coloured Persons* (Philadelphia: Presbyterian Board of Education, 1835), preface.
8. Paul's Letter to the Colossians 4:1.

Holy Scriptures and to encourage them to seek their soul's salvation' and he reminded the masters that they will be shown no more favour by God than their slaves just because of their position. 'God is no respecter of persons' he wrote.

The duties prescribed for servants or slaves are, not surprisingly a call to submission and, if necessary patient suffering, in the hope of a later reward from God. St Paul's injunction 'slaves obey your masters' is featured strongly and slaves are urged to try to please even difficult and harsh masters. He comes down very hard on lying, deception and stealing, some of the very tools of survival that many employed on the plantations. 'It is contrary to the will of God', he wrote, 'for servants either to run away or harbor a runaway. The servant who always abides at home at faithful service, fares better a thousand fold than he who runs away.' That must have been music to the ears of most 'slave-owners' who could conveniently ignore the first part of the duties.[9]

Charles Colcock Jones, though he had no blood relationship to Scotland, exemplified Knoxian values both in his plantation work and his missionary work. He saw the running of the plantation as a godly enterprise of good order and discipline. Not one to indulge in the sadistic excesses of many 'slave-owners' he nonetheless maintained strict discipline amongst the enslaved on his plantations, and did not shirk from approving punishment that was inevitably harsh. He took as his motto Calvin's insistence that the nobility (and such he was on his own lands) 'spread the true religion amongst their dependants'. This too had to be done in an orderly way. The travel writer Frederick Law Olmstead observed in 1862:

> In the county of Liberty in Georgia a Presbyterian minister has for many years been employed exclusively in labouring for the moral enlightenment of the slaves. I believe that in no other district has there been displayed a general and long-continued interest in the spiritual well-being of the negroes.[10]

One of Jones' greatest frustrations was that the sanctity of Christian marriage, in which he strongly believed, was made impossible by laws

---

9. Jones, *Catechism of Scripture,* pp. 127 ff.
10. F. L. Olmsted,. *The Cotton Kingdom* (New York; Mason Brothers) 1862. Cited in Clarke, *Wrestlin' Jacob,* p. xii.

in most of the Southern states that did not legally recognise any slave unions. Above all he deplored any separation by 'sale or purchase'. He recognised that economic reasons for the breakup of families were the most immoral of motives. However in 1857, under economic pressure, Jones decided to sell a 'troublesome' slave named Jane. At first it was decided that her whole family was to be sold with her but again financial considerations led to part of the family being kept and Jane, who died shortly afterwards, never saw them again. It was of course an all too common practice throughout slavery, but it exposed the impossibility of an owner and Christian minister holding these two roles ethically together.[11]

Thomas Smyth (1808-1873) – Pastor and Scholar

Revd Thomas Smyth, Minister of the Second Presbyterian Church in Charleston, has been described by his biographer, Erskine Clarke, as 'A Moderate Southernor'.[12] Smyth was born of an English father and Scottish mother, and brought up originally in Belfast, for which he retained a great affection. Smyth's family came to Charleston in 1830, and after two years study at Princeton, he became supply minister in Second Presbyterian. His whole ministry was with that church, and one that spanned well beyond the Civil War until his death in 1873. Unlike Jones, whom he first met as a student in Princeton, he was a shy and retiring man, given to long scholarly sermons, and more at home with his library of 15,000 books than with people. Smyth was a prolific writer of scholarly pamphlets and books on ecclesiastical order, theology, philosophy and science and a key figure in the Charleston Literary and Philosophical Society. Thomas Smyth shared Charles Jones' concern for the religious education of slaves – the two collaborated on this in the Presbyterian church structures, especially in the teeth of a great deal of civic opposition. His sister Margaret had married John Adger, and the Smyth and Adger families lived close by each other. It was no accident that the bid to persuade the great, if not always the good, in Charleston in 1847, to allow Adger to minister to a separate black congregation emerged from Second

---

11. Clarke, *Dwelling Place*. 349-353.
12. Erskine Clarke, 'Thomas Smyth, Moderate of the Old South', ThD Dissertation, Union Seminary, Richmond 1970. *American National Biography* pp. 331-32.

Presbyterian. Smyth gave quiet support to the movement for religious education for enslaved people, as he did to the movement for mission in Africa – missionaries were commissioned in his church, and he often preached the valedictory sermon.

In the same way as Jones and the Adgers, Smyth had severe reservations about slavery. He described it as an 'evil' which he claimed that 'God would remove in his own time', a position he held to throughout the turbulent decades of the 1830s, 1840s, and 1850s. In 1850 he published a book *The Unity of the Human Race*. It was a long and detailed scholarly work of several hundred pages. He took four years to research it and its conclusions, radical for South Carolina, were that scripture, reason and science all supported the thesis in the title. 'Our Saviour', he argued, 'traced all mankind to the original stock.' He continued his findings:

> The Scriptures teach that all races of men, black or white, African and Caucasian, were subsequently dispersed from one postdiluvian stock, that all are sinners, and that there is but one name under Heaven by which any man can be saved, and they require the gospel of this grace and mercy to be preached to every creature.[13]

There could hardly be a more eloquent and tightly argued response, not only to those who justified slavery, but also the same justification for the doctrine of racial segregation in a later era. It was in fact a response to a series of lectures by a Professor Agassiz to the Literary and Philosophical Society in the city. Had it been widely distributed it might well have compromised Smyth's ministry, if not at least his continuing stay in Charleston. As it was, he found himself being accused publicly, not least by other ministers, of being 'A Partisan of the Philadelphia Cabal' and 'an abolitionist'.[14]

Unlike Jones, Thomas Smyth owned no slaves and made it clear he did not wish to do so, although his wife Margaret Adger had inherited

---

13. Thomas Smyth, *The Unity of the Human Race Proved to be the Doctrine of Scripture, Reason, and Science* (New York: George Putman, 1849), pp. xvi and 43.
14. Thomas Smyth and Louisa Cheves Stoney, *Autobiographical Notes, Letters and Reflections* (Charleston: Walker, Evans & Cogswell, 1914), pp. 175, 215.

some. But his international contacts brought on him a wave of hostility because of his perceived accommodation to the system. When a delegation came from the new Free Church of Scotland which had split from the Church of Scotland in 1843, he welcomed them and assisted with a modest contribution from sympathisers in the city. For raising money in Charleston for them he then became embroiled in a dispute which brought the anger both of American and Scottish abolitionists. Both the American and Foreign Anti-Slavery Society and the Glasgow Emancipation Society issued the strongest rebukes, calling for the rejection of any 'blood money' from slavery. The former, in a letter to the Scottish delegation commended the Free Church for their courageous stand against the 'tyranny' of a state church but reminded them:

> You are now sojourning in the house of the serpent (of slavery. We have, it is true, his slime and his folds in the North but his head and fangs are in the South. Are you in no danger of fascination of his eye? ... You are at war with oppression and you come to us for the sinews of war. Can you suppose that the wages of iniquity are of any value to you?[15]

As Smyth became more defensive of the Southern situation, and more under attack in Scotland and Ireland, he turned to his friend Thomas Chalmers, the best known churchman in Scotland. Both men shared a conservatism and regard for order in religion and in society where the Calvinist and Knoxian values of the 'two realms' ruled. Smyth was later to write a defence of Calvin's life and principles.[16] Chalmers appreciated the order of the old South, and Smyth admired Chalmers' vision of a 'Godly Commonwealth' for Scotland based on the ideal of Calvin's Geneva. Chalmers as a young minister in Fife had pressed his local Presbytery to send a petition to the British Parliament in 1815, demanding the abolition of the French slave trade as a condition of the peace treaty between the two nations. There was no doubt that he agreed that slavery was an evil system.

---

15. Whyte, *'Send Back the Money': The Free Church of Scotland and American Slavery* (Cambridge: James Clarke, 2012) p. 26.
16. Thomas Smyth, *Calvin and his Enemies: A Memoir of the Life, Character and Principles of Calvinism* (Philadelphia: Presbyterian Press, 1856).

Yet he assured Smyth that war too was a great evil, but did not warrant the excommunication of soldiers. 'Slave-owners', in his view, should be judged by the church for their behaviour towards enslaved people, but the fact of being an 'owner' was not a warrant for condemnation. Taking the doctrine of 'two kingdoms' of church and state, he went so far as to argue that in good time we would see an end to slavery. 'Christianity', he claimed, 'does not deal with political and civic institutions but it deals with individuals and ecclesiastical institutions.' This was music to Smyth's ears, since it gave support for him to work to mitigate slavery and offer the benefits of religion to enslaved people and free African Americans, whilst avoiding any obligation to call for their emancipation, that he and Chalmers believed to be an inevitable and desirous work of God in good time.[17]

The refusal of Smyth to support the excommunication from the church of any who 'owned' enslaved people alienated him from old friends in the Presbyterian Church in Ireland, which took a much firmer line on 'slave-owners' than the leadership of the Free Church of Scotland. Revd Isaac Nelson, a leading figure in both the church and the Belfast Anti-Slavery Society ensured that Smyth was denied a seat at the Irish Assembly, a fact that caused much glee from the celebrated self-liberated former slave and abolitionist orator Frederick Douglass. Douglass had been sent from America to challenge the Free Church to 'Send Back the Money' and cut links with 'slave-holding churches' and although never meeting Smyth he pursued him relentlessly in the press as both men travelled through Scotland and Ireland.

In 1846 shortly after his visit to Scotland and Ireland Smyth was part of an American delegation at the newly formed Evangelical Alliance in London. The Alliance fiercely debated the issue of whether it could include in its membership any church that admitted 'slave-owners' to communion. There was some doubt whether Smyth or John Adger, recently returned from mission work in Armenia, would be allowed to participate. They were permitted to speak and Smyth took the same position as Thomas Chalmers had done in the Free Church, affirming that they were all wishing to see slavery come to

---

17. I. Whyte, *'Send Back the Money'*, pp. 43-56. George Shepperson, 'Notes and Documents: Thomas Chalmers, the Free Church of Scotland, and the South', *Journal of Southern History* Vol 3(1951), pp. 517-37.

an end, but that this was a political matter and had no place in church courts.[18]

James Henley Thornwell (1812-1862) – Theologian and Leader

The third figure who was crucial to Presbyterian involvement with religious education was the theologian and Moderator in 1847 of the General Assembly of the Presbyterian Church, James Henley Thornwell. Thornwell, son of a plantation overseer, studied at South Carolina College and Harvard, and was minister of the Presbyterian Church in Lancaster, South Carolina, from 1835 to 1837 and in Columbia briefly in 1837 before teaching in his old college and then in the new Colombia Seminary in whose inception he played a strong role alongside both Jones and Smyth.

Thornwell was one of the founding editors in 1847 of the *Southern Presbyterian Review*, contributing nearly 30 articles, and from 1855 he edited the *Southern Quarterly Review*. In both journals he held extensive discussions on the issue of slavery, with detailed justifications and also instructions to servants and masters. In 1847 he inserted in the journal a sermon preached in 1850 commending 'The Baptism of Servants', which gave a biblical warrant for slavery. He wrote:

> The Institution of slavery is continually alluded to in the scriptures, recognised as an existing condition of human society, and spoken of without the slightest mark of divine approbation.
>
> He who cannot look on sin with allowance, took slaveholders to be his special friends ... revealed to them in an especial manner his holy will, appointed some of them to be his prophets and representatives on earth ... and closed the volume of inspiration, which condemns all sin, without one word of censure pronounced against the system.[19]

---

18. *Evangelical Alliance: Report of the Proceedings of the Conference held at Freemasons Hall, London from Aug 19 to Sep 2* (London: Partridge & Oakley, 1847), pp 304-09.
19. J.H. Thornwell, 'The Baptism of Servants', *Southern Presbyterian Review*, 6 (1847), p. 64.

Thornwell has been credited as having influenced in his youth not only by Calvinism, but by 'Scottish Common Sense Realism'.[20] Most, but not all, philosophers of the Scottish Enlightenment saw slavery as unjustified in a civilised society, although Scotland profited economically from it. Thornwell saw it as a curse and not a blessing, but he accepted that the doctrine of divine providence required that this 'natural evil' was a given. God could extract a blessing from it, in bringing the benefits of Christianity to those who had been taken from Africa, 'while their brethren at home are worshippers of the devil'. Therefore the 'two kingdoms' theology of Calvinism enabled him, as other Presbyterians, to embrace paternalism by exemplary personal behaviour and the missionary imperative within the given structures of slavery. He wrote and preached extensively on the duties of masters and servants towards each other in an ordered framework, putting theological flesh on the bones of Charles Colcock Jones' work, and focussing on the necessity of baptism, Christian teaching, and opportunities for worship, given to enslaved and free African Americans.[21]

In these instructions and in the many pamphlets which he wrote, he rejected the idea that slavery was more than a 'supposed evil' and that the holding of slaves was sinful. On the other hand he expressed strong concern about the 'abuses' and 'evils' of slavery and in his strictures on *The Rights and Duties of Masters* he went even further than Charles Colcock Jones. He began by claiming that 'the destiny of the negro race, for wise ends. has been bound onto our own – we are constituted their guardians, their teachers, their civilisers'. For this reason he rejected many powers that 'masters' assumed. The 'master', for Thornwell 'has no property in his slave as he has in the ox or the swine ... his soul, his limbs, his heart lie in the slave'. All that the master has a right to is 'a claim to (the slave's) services'. He argued that

---

20. The Scottish 'Common Sense' philosophy came out of the thinking of the Scottish Enlightenment n the eighteenth century. It held that all people had experiences that provided intuitively certain principles of sound moral and religious beliefs.
21. Erskine Clarke, 'James Henley Thornwell', *South Carolina Encyclopedia* (Columbia, SC: University of South Carolina Institute for Southern Studies, June 2016): Marilyn J. Westerkamp, 'James Henley Thornwell, Pro-Slavery Spokesman within a Calvinist Faith', *South Carolina Historical Magazine,* Vol. 87 (Jan. 1986), pp. 57-58.

the New Testament injunction 'masters give your servants that that is just and equal' makes the slave 'a member of the family, although the lowest one', and he argued that the relationship should be compared to 'the vassals of the Middle Ages rather than the serfs of Russia'. Masters should seek for slaves 'the greatest amount of happiness that their condition will admit' and 'masters' who treat their slaves cruelly should be disciplined by the church.[22]

Although, in company with others, Thornwell saw the issue of slavery as a political and social one to be separated from the church's spiritual realm of authority, he was critical of the political powers in not giving protection to the enslaved in several areas. Marriage should be respected – and no families should be split up by sale. The recent law in South Carolina preventing the teaching of slaves to read Thornwell called 'disgraceful' and he and Charles Colcock Jones campaigned unsuccessfully to persuade the legislature to rescind it.

This ban of course had severe consequences for the biblical education of the enslaved and limited it to the hearing of teaching and preaching. As with others Thornwell saw the evangelism of slaves as the most crucial duty of masters as of the mission of the church. In 'Slavery and the Religious Instruction of the Coloured People' (cited at the start of this chapter) he rated baptism crucial as opening the way to salvation. This should neither be neglected because of the ignorance of the candidate in religious matters nor even if the enslaved person declined it for him or his family. It is reminiscent of General Gordon who later in the century baptised his troops in China with a hosepipe, whether they wanted it or not, to ensure their spiritual welfare!

Jones, Smyth and Thornwell recognised the need for African Americans to have their own places of worship. This was the precursor of segregation in church (Martin Luther King's dictum that 11.00 on a Sunday morning was the most segregated hour of the week) but it was also a recognition that worship in white churches was often unacceptable to black people. There were earlier attempts to establish black churches but a landmark event took place in May 1850 with the building by white Presbyterians and Episcopalians of Zion Church in

---

22. J.H. Thornwell, *The Rights and Duties of Masters: A Sermon Preached at the Dedication of a Church erected in Charleston, South Carolina for the Benefit and Instruction of the Colored Population* (Charleston: Walker & James, 1850).

Charleston to house a black congregation. Such a venture had been hotly contested in Charleston society, many of whom thought it a dangerous departure. By this time there was a strong revulsion to any reform of slavery not just in the lee of rebellions but responding to the growing attempts of abolitionists throughout America to press for emancipation and to disseminate propaganda through the post. Zion Church in Anson Street was only achieved by huge compromises. It was to be supervised by Smyth's Second Presbyterian Church, white ministers were to be appointed to it (Smyth's brother-in-law was the first one) and although the opening sermon was preached by Thornwell on the text 'masters give to your servants that which is just and equal, knowing that ye have a master in heaven', the congregation at that service was entirely white, and it was clear that no abolitionist tinge was to be allowed in the church.

Thornwell's sermon spoke of the 'insane fury of the abolitionist philanthropy' that 'has aimed at stirring up insurrection in our midst' and 'threatens the utter ruin of this vast Republic'. Yet there was an admission that, although in his view the South were unjustly calumniated for slavery, 'to say that we have run into no extravagancies in our defence of slavery is to say that we are not angels but men'. The remainder of the sermon, which must have been the best part of two hours, was a justification of slavery as 'regulated liberty' resisting 'the social anarchy of communism and the political anarchy of licenciousness'. For Thornwell, God had permitted the phenomenon of slavery – it is a given and therefore not a sinful institution. He claimed:

> According to what is assigned to us in the tumult of the age, it is the maintenance of the principles upon which the security of social order and the development of humanity depends, in their application to the distinctive institutions which have provoked upon us the malediction of the world.[23]

Thornwell was the most conservative of the three mentioned, but he exemplified perfectly the dilemma in which more moderate Southern churchmen found themselves. The historian Eugene Genovese generously judged that Thornwell attempted 'to envision a Christian society that could reconcile – so far as possible in a world

---

23. Ibid.

haunted by evil – the conflicting claims of a social order with social justice and both with the freedom and dignity of the individual'. He would agree with the judgement of another scholar writing on these attempts to evangelise that, above all, the evangelists had to prove that their efforts posed no threat to slavery, to the South's way of life.[24]

In a sense those churchmen, and Presbyterians were in the vanguard, who tried to remain loyal Southerners and yet hold a vision of humanity and a zeal for saving souls that they believed to be a priority and a duty towards slaves, were caught in an impossible trap. As the nation lurched closer and closer towards Civil War, they were forced to take sides decisively, and in doing so lost much of their earlier vision and humanity. It was said of Charles Colcock Jones that, when he sent that family to the slave market in Savannah 1854, this above all marked his departure from earlier convictions about the evils of slavery to unwavering support of the South and human bondage. Several days before the guns at Fort Sumter rang out heralding the Civil War, Thomas Smyth received a letter from the Presbytery clerk, commending him for a robust theological defence of slavery in an article in a scientific journal, and promising that it provided unanswerable ammunition to use against the abolitionists.[25] Smyth remained committed to the Union until then but with the election of Lincoln, whom he hated, his loyalty became entirely with the South and the justification of Secession.

---

24. Albert Raboteau, *Slave Religion: The 'Invisible Institution' in the Antebellum South* (Oxford: Oxford University Press, 1978 p. 157.
25. Second Presbyterian Church Charleston, Session Minute Book 1852-1867, South Carolina Historical Society Manuscripts 428.04.01.

Chapter 7

Religion in the Memory of the Enslaved

A white preacher always told us to obey our masters and work hard and sing and when we die we go to heaven. Marse Tom didn't mind us singing in cabins at night, but we better not let him catch us prayin.

—William Moore, Texas[1]

On Sunday nights, a slave named Alan, used to come to Mr Gooch's estate for the purpose of exhorting and praying with his brother slaves, by whose instrumentality many of them had been converted. One evening Mr Gooch caught them all in a room, turned Allen out, and threatened his slaves with a hundred lashes each, if they ever brought him again.

—*A Narrative of the Adventures and Escape of Moses Roper from American Slavery*[2]

The publication in 1852 of Harriet Beecher Stowe's *Uncle Tom's Cabin* had the remarkable effect of lifting the veil on the reality of plantation slavery in the United States and throughout the English-speaking

---

1. Norman Yetman (ed.), *Memoirs from the Slave Narrative Collection* (Mineola, NY: Dover Thrift Publications, 2002), p. 94.
2. M. Roper. *A Narrative of the Adventures and Escape of Moses Roper from American Slavery* (Philadelphia: Merrihew & Gunn, 1838).

world. It has been credited with assisting the onset of the Civil War. Yet despite the passionate support of the author and her husband for abolition, it was a white perception, albeit a liberal one. Far less publicised were the accounts by African Americans who had liberated themselves from slavery, acquired literacy and achieved publication of their memoirs, but they reached a much more limited audience.

By the time that Mrs Stowe's novel was published, already enslaved people who had liberated themselves such as Henry Bibb in New York, Moses Roper and William Wells Brown in Philadelphia and James Pennington in London had turned their story into print. Perhaps the best known and most widely circulated was the narrative of Frederick Douglass, who became one of the most celebrated of anti-slavery advocates on both sides of the Atlantic.[3] In the half-century before the Emancipation Proclamation nearly a dozen first-hand accounts by African Americans went into print.

In the mid-twentieth century historians and archivists realised that very soon there would be no more opportunities to hear directly from those who had been born and raised in slavery. An extensive project was embarked upon in the 1930s to record the memories of people who were, in some cases, 80 or more years old. The voices of enslaved people were recorded, unvarnished by the accounts given to strangers (or any white persons) during slavery, no longer in the language necessary for protection and indeed survival. They became a rich source of witness to authentic experience, and enabled later generations to understand how enslaved men and women dealt with religion and many other things.

These accounts demonstrate that, despite the best and mainly sincere intentions of Reformed ministers such as Charles Colcock Jones, James Henley Thornwell and Thomas Smyth, and the concern for religious instruction and the nurturing of enslaved people in Christianity, philanthropic evangelism was very little reflected in the accounts from those on the Southern plantations. Their reminiscences cover a great variety of attitudes of 'masters' and 'mistresses' towards the use of religion in dealing with the men and women in their power.

At one end of the spectrum there was accommodation, encouragement and even facilitation of religion, though the last is reflected in only a few of the verbal accounts. At the other end there was all too much prohibition, interference and severe and cruel punishment,

---

3. F. Douglass, *Narrative of the Life of Frederick Douglass* (Boston, 1845).

meted out to those who showed any expression of religious thought or practice not specifically permitted or enforced. In between were a myriad of restrictions and controls, ensuring a careful selection of biblical passages, and the employment of ministers who often claimed divine approval for the obedience of the enslaved. And throughout it all, often at great risk, there was a very different, courageous, but vibrant, independent religious expression from enslaved people, that survives to this day in African American Christianity, and was developed against all the odds in the time of slavery.

Two – Faced Masters and Mistresses

A parodied hymn attributed to Lewis and Milton Clarke,[4] contains these verses:

> Come saints and sinners, hear me tell,
> How pious priests whip Jack and Nell,
> And women buy, and children sell,
> And preach all sinners down to hell
> And sing of heavenly union.
>
> They'll talk of heaven and Christ's reward,
> And bind his image with a cord
> And scold and swing the lash abhorred,
> And sell their brother in the Lord
> To handcuffed heavenly union
>
> They'll read and sing a sacred song
> And make a prayer both loud and long,
> And teach the right and do the wrong;
> Hailing the brother, sister throng,
> With words of heavenly union.
>
> We wonder how such saints can sing,
> Or praise the Lord upon the wing,

---

4. Milton Clarke, *Narrative of the Sufferings of Lewis and Milton Clarke, Sons of a Soldier of the Revolution, During a Captivity of More than Twenty Years among the Slaveholders of Kentucky, One of the So Called Christian States of North America* (Boston: Bela Marsh, 1846), appendix and notes.

Who roar and scold and whip and sting,
And to their slaves and mammon cling,
In guilty conscience union.

Milton Clarke of Kentucky, a son of an enslaved woman and a Scottish weaver, found himself a bondsman, despite his father's will that he should be free, and before the old man died his estate was sent to auction. Milton was himself sold to Joseph Logan, a tanner in Lexington, Kentucky, whom he described as 'a tall, lank, grey-eyed, hard-hearted, cruel wretch; but in good and regular standing in the Episcopalian church'. From the description of Logan's 'punishments' Milton Clarke shows, even by the standards of slavery, new depths of psychotic sadism were reached. Silas Jackson recalled his owner Tom Ashbie in Virginia as 'a meaner man was never born – brutal, wicked, and hard'. He told that when Ashbie's father went to the slave cabins one night where, at a secret prayer meeting, he heard one slave ask God to change the heart of the master and deliver him from slavery. Jackson reported: 'before the next day the man disappeared, no one ever seeing him again'. A little delayed, the older Ashbie confessed on his deathbed to the Baptist minister that he had killed Zeke for praying, and that he was going to hell.[5]

William Wells Brown, who later visited Scotland as a lecturer on the anti-slavery circuit, recalled driving his master's carriage to church on a Sunday and seeing a local Baptist deacon 'in good and regular standing' brutally pursuing a slave with a whip, having earlier nearly beaten to death Delphia, one of the enslaved women who was a member of the same church. Julia Brown in Georgia recalled life in the Mitchell family who took them to church. She slept on the floor in the house winter and summer with nothing but a flimsy dress, as her mistress 'took delight in callin' slaves. She'd lash us with a cowhide whip. Slaves were treated in most cases like cattle.'[6]

Moses Roper described his 'owner' in South Carolina as a Mr Gooch, a member of the Baptist Church. He was an extremely cruel man, and most of the enslaved opted for the Methodist Church, 'thinking him to be a very bad example of what a Christian should

---

5. Yetman, *Memoirs*, p. 74.
6. William Wells Brown, *Narrative of William Wells Brown, A Fugitive Slave, Written by Himself* (Boston: Anti-Slavery Office, 1845), pp. 38-39. Norman R. Yetman (ed.), *Voices from Slavery: 100 Authentic Slave Narratives* (Mineola, NY: Dover Publications, 1970), p. 47.

be'. Roper described the horrific tortures that Gooch inflicted on his slaves, particularly female ones. His descriptions in his account are bad enough, but he observed that during the eighteen months he spent on that plantation 'the scenes that I witnessed and experienced are not at all fitted for these pages'. Roper elaborated with the instance quoted at the beginning of the chapter. On another occasion he described a Mr Bell, a Methodist, who had hired a young former domestic slave from another plantation to hoe three-quarters of an acre of cotton in South Carolina on a Saturday. The young man couldn't complete the task that day, and continued for a few rows on the Sunday. For this he was flogged to death for breaking the Sabbath. 'So much', declared Roper cynically, 'for the regard of this Methodist for the observance of the Sabbath'.[7]

James Pennington (1807-70), the blacksmith turned Presbyterian minister, later to be a key figure in the abolitionist cause, particularly referred to one of his cruellest masters as an Episcopalian as he described the 'punishment' of a 'deep and pious exemplary slave, an elderly man, who had a misunderstanding with the overseer'. As the whip was being laid on by the master and his son in the presence of his 5year-old daughter, Pennington observed that the man was 'articulating in a low tone of voice: I listened at the intervals between the stripes, and lo! He was praying'.[8]

Selective Biblical Teaching

Many masters were to limit the teachings of the Bible to those passages which justified slavery. But few were as crude and extreme as that found in the account by Solomon Northup, the free man who was kidnapped in Washington in 1841. Northup's story has been dramatised in the film *Twelve Years a Slave*. He dedicated his manuscript to Harriet Beecher Stowe as 'another key to *Uncle Tom's Cabin*'. When on a plantation in Louisiana owned by a deacon of the local church, Peter Tanner, he remembered the man confining slaves to the stocks for easing their thirst by eating water melon on the Sabbath day. Northup commented that Tanner was 'an impressive

---

7. Roper, *Narrative of the Adventures and Escape of Moses Roper.from American Slavery* (Philadelphia: 1838).
8. James W. C. Pennington, *The Fugitive Blacksmith* (London: Charles Gilpin, 1849), pp. 10-11.

commentator on the New Testament'. He was 'in the habit of reading the Bible to his slaves on the Sabbath, but in a somewhat different spirit'. The first Sunday that Northup spent on the plantation, Tanner made great play of Jesus' words in Luke 11:47 about those who know the masters' will and didn't do it being beaten with many stripes. Ignoring the metaphorical meaning, Tanner went on to justify his literalism by threatening 'the nigger who don't take care shall be beaten with many stripes. "Many" signifies "a great many." Forty, a Hundred, a Hundred and fifty lashes: that's Scripture.'[9]

Most of the accounts were not quite as extreme as Northup's one, but the place offered in the white churches were not exactly conducive to Christian nurture. Worshippers were racially segregated in most places, with enslaved people and free blacks in the gallery or at the back. Lorenzo Ezell's experience was perhaps more extreme in rural North Carolina:

> The Old Massa, he insisted us go to church. De Baptist church built behind the pulpit for culled folks, with de dirt floor and split log seat for de women folks, but most of de men folks stands or knells on the floor. Dey used to call dat de coop. De white preacher back to us, but iffen he want to, he turn round and talk to us a while.[10]

It isn't recorded what the preacher talked about to them, but William Moore in Texas recalled that 'Some Sundays we went to church some place. We always liked to go any place. A white preacher told us to obey our masters and work hard and sing, and when we die we go to heaven.'[11]

Of course most saw through this, and even told it in later life with a twinkle. After a description of the difficulty of eking out provisions by stealing a chicken or a pig from the plantation, Richard Carruthers

---

9. Solomon Northup, *Twelve Years a Slave: Narrative of Solomon Northup, A Citizen of New York, Kidnapped in Washington in 1841, and Rescued in 1853, from a Cotton Plantation near the Red River in Louisiana* (Auburn, AL: Derby & Miller, 1853), pp. 127-28. Norman Yetman (ed.), *When I was a Slave, Memoirs from the Slave Narrative Collection*, (Mineola, New York:Dover Publications 2002) dedication page and p. 94.
10. Yetman (ed.), *Voices from Slavery*, p. 112.
11. Yetman (ed.), *When I was a Slave*, p. 94.

in rural Texas remembered: 'When the white preacher come to preach and pickup his Bible, and claim he gettin' the text right out from the good Book, and he preach the Lord say, don't you niggers steal chickens from your missus. Don't you steal your master's hogs. That would be all he would preach.'[12]

Harriet Jacobs in North Carolina described how Revd Mr Pike, an Episcopalian minister or preacher who made sure that his biblical allusions suited her 'master', gave elaborate signs of piety and prayer, 'brushed his hair until it stood upright and in deep, solemn tones began':

> Hearken, ye servants! Give strict heed to my words. You are rebellious spirits. Your hearts are filled with all maimer (sic!) of evil ... God will surely punish you if you don't forsake your wicked ways. He then elaborated this with charges of idleness, drunkenness, and theft, the old convenient myths that comforted the 'slave-owners'.

Pike continued:

> Although your masters may not find you out, God sees you, and he will punish you. Your old master and your young master – your old mistress and your young mistress. If you disobey your earthly master, you offen your heavenly master. You must obey God's commandments. When you go from here, don't stop at the corners of the streets to talk, but go directly home.

Harriet's comment on this ridiculous performance was: 'We went home, highly amused at brother Pike's gospel teaching, and we determined to hear him again. I went the next Sabbath evening and heard pretty much a repetition of the last performance.'[13]

An enslaved but literate person in Wayne County, North Carolina, spelt out the frustration when he wrote to the white preacher:

---

12. Yetman (ed.), *Voices from Slavery*, p. 53.
13. Harriet Jacobs, 'Incidents in the Life of a Slave Girl', in Yuval Taylor (ed.), *I was Born a Slave: An Anthology of Slave Narratives* (Edinburgh: Playback Press Canongate, 1999), Vol. 2, pp. 587-88.

> Master John, I want permission if you pleas to speak a word to you … in the first place I want you to tell me the reason you always preach to white folks, and keep your back to us. if I should ask you what must I do to be saved, perhaps you would tell me pray let the bible be my guide, this would do very well if we could read. I have been more fortunate, than the most of the black people. I can read and write. If God sent you to preach to sinners did he direct you to keep your face constantly to the white people or is it because they give you money? Did God tell you to have your meeting in houses large enough to hold the white folks, and let the black people stand in the sun and rain?[14]

In Genovese's research, Presbyterian preachers do not feature well. There is a story told of a young white minister who began his sermon with: 'Primarily, we must postulate the existence of a deity', to which an elderly enslaved man responded 'Yes Lord, dats so. Bless de Lord.' Revd Samuel Agnew, Presbyterian minister in Mississippi, noted contemptuously in his diary that he had visited a 'negro prayer meeting' where he experienced for the first time black preaching from what he called 'Afric's ebony sons'. He complained about the 'King's English' being 'mercilessly cut up', concluded that 'there is not much faith in the negroe' and he sped home as quickly as he could.[15]

But of course enslaved folk saw through the convenient tailoring of religion to reflect the acceptable pattern of Southern norms. Andrew Moss in Georgia wryly claimed:

> White folks make a heap o' fun of de colored folks for all time prayin'. Sometime, say you was a slave and you get down to pray in de field or de side of de road, and Marster come along and see a slave on his knees. He say 'what are you praying about?' and you say ' Marster, I'se just prayin' to Jesus 'cause I wants to go to Heaven when I dies.' And Marster says, 'You's my Negro. I get you to Heaven. Get up offen your knees' De white folks what owned slaves thought

---

14. Jones, *African Americans and the Churches*, p. 111.
15. Agnew Diary, 31 Dec. 1865, cited in Genovese, *Roll, Jordan, Roll*, pp. 204-05.

that when they get to Heaven de colored folks would be dere to wait on 'em."[16]

Limitations on Praying, Religion and Movement

Those in control the lives of others have always been anxious about their charges getting together in association and gaining strength in questioning their lot. The fear of many white 'owners' that allowing gatherings of the enslaved for worship would lead, at the very least, to the comfort of mass uncontrolled expressions of feeling, and at worst a resolve to be free, was not unfounded. Those who led rebellion at this time drew heavily on biblical authority, and inspired others to see that oppression and bondage were never justified in scripture, and that freedom was the invitation given by the prophets and by Jesus.

On most plantations worship was strictly in the hands of white leaders, even when enslaved people were able to take part through singing and, in a segregated way, receive communion. This was so on Robert Shepherd's plantation in Georgia, whose owner, a Methodist lay preacher, shared the sermons with two Baptist ministers. Robert recalled with considerable satisfaction the three services that he attended.

> De biggest meeting house crowds came when dey had baptizin' and dat was right often. Dey dammed up de crick on Saturday so it would be deep enough on Sunday and dey done de baptizin' before they preached at de three o'clock service. At dem baptizin's dere was all kinds of shoutin,' and dey would sig "Roll Jordan Roll" "De Living Waters" and " Lord I'se Coming Home."[17]

On the plantation regulations varied over the permitting of expression. William Moore recalled that his master had no objection to singing in the cabins, but strictly prohibited prayers, presumably because the supplications might not be to his liking, and could encourage others.[18]

---

16. Yetman (ed.), *When I was a Slave*, p. 98.
17. Yetman (ed.), *Voices from Slavery*, p. 266.
18. Yetman (ed.), *When I was a Slave*, p. 94.

It might be assumed that hymns, with their public utterances and looking to better times, rather than prayers, would cause more concern to 'slave-owners'. Accounts make it clear that group prayers were seen as the most subversive. But even quiet individual prayers were often viewed as a threat. Some 'slave-owners' allowed passes to attend meetings for worship, but there were many examples cited of those who were caught without passes by the 'patrollers' and received severe floggings.

Mary Ella Grandberry from Alabama spoke of the one church near her plantation that they were only allowed to go to accompanied by white people. She recalled that once there:

> Us didn't get no pleasure outen goin' to church, 'since we weren't allowed to say nothin'. We wer'nt even allowed to talk with anyone from another farm. Iffen you did, you got one of the worst whippin's of your life. After freedom Massa Jim told us dat dey was 'fraid we'd get together and try to run to the North, and that was why dey didn't want us gettin' together talkin'[19]

It is true that many 'slave-owners' felt that any communication with others outside the plantation which was not strictly overseen by them was a potential threat to security and control. There was undoubtedly some basis for this, although at times it was paranoia.

Christian Benevolence

Stories of kind and liberal behaviour by Christian 'slave-owners' do feature in these accounts, but they are not common, and contrast sharply with the propaganda that justified 'The Peculiar Institution'. Clearly there were some 'slave-owners' who tried to practise their faith, and in this way ran the risk of being vilified or worse. Marriah Hines from Virginia recalled about her 'master':

> He was a true Christian man and I mean he sure lived up to it. We didn't even have to work on Sundays, even in the house, or in bad weather or when it got real cold. He never did force us to go to Church if we didn't want to.

---
19. Yetman (ed.), *Voices from Slavery*, p. 145.

She recalled that, in contrast with other plantations, they were given good food and clothing 'plenty to keep us comfortable'.

Unusually she related that there were 'no coloured overseers to whip us, nor no white ones'. Every evening there were prayers said for the enslaved, and on a Wednesday a prayer meeting with singing and praying was permitted. Not surprisingly Marriah related: 'cause Master was good and kind to us, some of the other white folks used to call him "nigger lover". He didn't pay that no mind though.'[20]

Often the accounts contrast the benevolent situation on their plantation with the fate of others on a nearby one, but hardly ever the other way round. John Brown, in Alabama, a state which in 1832 instituted heavy legal penalties for anyone teaching literacy to slaves, reported that his master taught him and others to read and write. He described Sunday as 'a great day around the plantation'. Work was light, and everyone got ready for the church meeting in the yard in front of the house.

> Master John's wife would start the meeting with a prayer and then would come the singing – the old timey songs. But white folks on the next plantation would lick (flog) their slaves for trying to do like we did. No praying there, and no singing.[21]

Anthony Dawson in Oklahoma had an 'owner' who was from of Jewish ancestry yet he described him as 'a fine Christian'. Dawson told that Levi Dawson:

> Let us niggers have preachings and prayers, and would give us a parole to go ten or fifteen miles to a camp meeting, and stay two or three days with nobody but Uncle John to stand for us. Mostly we had white preachers, but when we had a black preacher, that was heaven.[22]

Ria Sorrell, when interviewed at the age of 97, made a clear distinction between the meanness and cruelty of her mistress in North Carolina, and her husband, who wouldn't sell anyone and insisted on

---

20. Ibid., pp. 166-67.
21. Ibid., pp. 45, 46.
22. Ibid., p. 95.

decent food and shelter. She reckoned that he was going to heaven, but was very doubtful about 'Missus'. Holidays from work were freely given, with time off in addition, to enable them to work their own land, and a week at Christmas. Ria described him as a 'father' who brought food to the cabins, unknown to his wife. 'He said that he was a Christian, and believed in giving us a chance. Some nights Marster would come to our cabins, call us all in to one of them, and pray with us.'[23]

John Thomson in Maryland gave accounts of the contrast between the violence inflicted on the slaves of some plantations and his own experience latterly, with those to whom he was hired. In that part of the state several 'owners' combined to build a church for the enslaved and he particularly commended a Mr Compton for whom he worked for a year:

> A kind master; feeding and clothing well, and seldom beating his slaves … his slaves were all religious and much attached to their master and mistress. They were allowed to hold their prayer meetings unmolested, in their own quarters, and I felt thankful that I had once again got among Christians.

Yet there was a sting in the tail, amidst such benevolence. The Comptons, as many plantation owners, were to over-reach their finances, and the debts incurred meant that the easiest and perhaps only way of remedying this was to sell their enslaved folk. And so it was that out of 100 workers, 60 were sent to town to pack tobacco, incarcerated in a warehouse and loaded on a ship for the Southern slave markets.[24]

Doing their own Thing

In the prominently Presbyterian area of Ashville, North Carolina, W.L. Bost reflected:

> Us niggers never have the chance to go to Sunday School or Church. The white folks feared for niggers to get any

---

23. Ibid., pp. 294-95.
24. J. John Thomson, *The Life of John Thomson, A Fugitive Slave* (Worcester, MA: John Thomson, 1856), pp. 40-42.

> religion and education, but I reckon somethin' inside just told us about God and that there was a better place hereafter. We would sneak off and have prayer meetin'. Sometimes the patterrollers [patrollers], hired to control movements of the enslaved] catch us and beat us good, but that didn't keep us from tryin' ... Us poor niggers never allowed to learn anything. All the reading they ever hear is when they was carried through the Big Bible. The massa say that keeps slaves in their place.[25]

With courage and resilience many enslaved people took time out of their small ration of sleep late at night to gather for worship. Richard Carruthers recalled:

> Us niggers used to have a praying ground down in the hollow and sometime we came out of the field, between eleven and twelve at night, scorchin' and burnin' up with nothin' to eat, and we wants to ask the good Lord to have mercy. We put grease in a snuff pan or bottle and make a lamp. We takes a pine torch too, and goes down to the hollow to pray. Some gets so joyous they starts to holler loud and we have to stop up they mouth. I see niggers get so full of the Lord, and so happy they drops unconscious.[26]

Marriah Hines' account is somewhat different.

> On our plantation we had general prayer meeting every Wednesday at church 'Cause some of the masters didn't like the way we slaves carried on, we would turn pots down and tubs to keep the sound from going out. Den we would have a good time, shouting, singing, and praying just like we pleased. The paterrollers didn't pay us much attention, 'cause they knew how Master let us do. Dey would say nasty things about Master 'cause he let us do what we s do like we did.[27]

---

25. Yetman (ed.), *Voices from Slavery*, pp. 36, 37.
26. Ibid., p. 53.
27. Ibid., p. 167.

Enslaved people forged out of their darkness a remarkable pattern of worship which enabled their humanity to survive, their faith to be nourished, their hope against all the odds to remain alive and their community to remain strong. It is into that heritage that today's African Americans have entered and found powerful roots of community and Christian expression. It is therefore not surprising that in all the accounts of the experience of religion in the personal testimonies that were used in the campaign against slavery in the nineteenth century and in those given to researchers in the mid-twentieth, there is little insight into those private moments when enslaved people were able to express their deepest feelings in worship. Even when it was safe to speak of these things, few would wish to entrust them to white academic interviewers.

Enslaved men and women found in worship on their own terms a coping mechanism of making the unending darkness of slavery bearable. It restored their humanity and sense of self-worth. For a brief and often risky time, they broke free not just of the physical but also of the spiritual control of others. But it was much more than that. Even those who could not discover the printed word of the Bible could hear the stories from those who had read them. They would be strengthened by the Old Testament prophetic tradition in which figures such as Amos and Micah called for God's justice and condemnation of those who oppressed the weak and the 'other'. They learned of the radical message of Jesus as the breaker of barriers, and above all they could not be prevented from confrontation with a God who delivered the enslaved Israelites from Egypt.

Chapter 8

Against the Odds – Two Self-Liberated Women in a Male Era

While the race is sold of all their rights – has not God given to all his creatures the same rights?. I knew Jesus. Then I learned that I was a human being.
—Sojourner Truth, Oct. 1856

I had crossed the line. I was free but there was no one to welcome me to the land of freedom. I was a stranger in a strange land; and my home, after all, was down in Maryland, because my father, my mother, my brothers, and sisters and friends were there. But I was free, and they should be free. I would make a home in the North and bring them there, God helping me.
—Harriet Tubman on her self-liberation, related by Sarah H. Bradford 1869[1]

---

1. Sarah Bradford (b. 1818) was an earlier biographer of Harriet Tubman. She relied on eyewitness accounts for her first book *Scenes in the Life of Harriet Tubman* (Auburn, NY, 1869) which was expanded into *Harriet Tubman: The Moses of her People* (Bedford, MA, 1886).

Women's Voices in Anti-Slavery

It is now widely recognised that, within much of the history of Christendom, women have been at best marginalised, and at worst abused and persecuted. They have also been excluded from full participation in the movements for social reform. The various societies on both side of the Atlantic that were formed in the nineteenth century to rid the world of the curse of slavery were no exception to this pattern.

William Wilberforce was resolute in his opposition to women taking any active part in the campaign to abolish British slavery, although some of his close associates such as Zachary Macaulay (1768-1838), the son of a Scottish minister, held a very different view. Even after British abolition, the London Congress meeting in 1840 to plan for abolition throughout the world allowed women delegates to attend, but decided that they could neither speak nor vote. Prominent American abolitionists such as Lucretia Mott and Elizabeth Cady, sent by their societies, were forced to sit silently in the upper gallery where they were joined by the editor of *The Liberator*, William Lloyd Garrison, and some other male delegates as a gesture of solidarity. The American Abolition Society had divided that same year on various issues, including the participation of women in its governance. All this makes it even more remarkable that several striking contributions to the struggle for freedom from slavery came from formerly enslaved women.

For years the first autobiographical account by a woman who had experienced the full weight of enslavement went unpublished. Harriet Jacobs learned to read and write in her early years in North Carolina before the state outlawed literacy for enslaved people in 1830. Resisting the sexual harassment of one of her 'owners', she hid in a swamp and then for seven years lived in a tiny space in her grandmother's house, constantly under threat of capture, until she was able to travel north. Harriet was persuaded by abolitionist friends to write *Incidents in the Life of a Slave Girl* under the pseudonym Linda Brent. She made the first draft in 1852 the same year that Harriet Beecher Stowe's *Uncle Tom's Cabin* became a best-seller, but an approach to Stowe for help was rebuffed. It took successful tours in England and America to finally secure a publisher in both countries in 1861-2. Most academic historians saw it as a fictional account, until research for a book in 1987 established conclusively that this was a genuine autobiography.² Other formerly enslaved women were to make a substantial contribution to the liberation of others in different ways, two of whom were to have reformed roots in their spiritual journeys.

Sojourner Truth (1797-1883)– The Prophetic Voice

In the Ohio *Anti-Slavery Bugle* in June 1851 the following report occurred of the Women's Rights Convention in Akron, Ohio.

> One of the most unique and interesting speeches was made by Sojourner Truth, an emancipated slave. It is impossible to transfer it to paper, or to convey any idea of the effect that it produced on the audience. Those only can appreciate it who saw her powerful form, her wholehearted earnest gestures, and listened to her strong and truthful tones. She came forward to the platform and addressing the President, said with great simplicity:
>
> May I say a few words. I want to say a few words about this matter. I am a woman's rights [Sic]. I have as much muscle as any man. I have plowed and reaped and husked and chopped and mowed, and can any man do more than that, I have heard much about the sexes being equal; I can carry as much as any man, and can eat as much too if I can get it. I am as strong as any man that is now. As for intellect, all I can say is, if women have a pint and man a quart – why can't she have her little pint full.
>
> You need not be afraid to give us our rights for fear we will take too much, for we can't take more than our pint will hold. The poor men seem to be all in confusion and don't know what to do. Why children, if you have woman's right, give it to her and you will feel better. You will have your own rights, and they won't be so much trouble. I can't read, but I can hear. I have heard the Bible and have learned that Eve caused man to sin. Well if woman upset the world, do give her a chance to set it right side up again.
>
> The Lady has spoken about Jesus, how he never spurned woman from him and she was right. When Lazarus died, Mary and Martha came to him with faith and besought him to raise their brother. And Jesus wept and Lazarus

---

2. Linda Brent, *Incidents in the Life of a Slave Girl* (1861).

came forth. And how came Jesus into the world? Through God who created him and women who bore him. Man where is your part? But the women are coming up, blessed be God, and a few men are coming up with them. But man is in a tight place, the poor slave is on him, and he is surely between a hawk and a buzzard.[3]

The speech was transcribed by a journalist and friend of the speaker, Revd Marius Robinson, who was in the audience at the time. Yet a myth that grew round a version published in 1863, which not only changed the speech, but ascribed the dialogue to a person brought up in the South, was far less polished, and ended with the rather submissive words 'bleeged to ye for hearin' on me, and now old Sojourner ha'nt s got nothing more to say'. Although that speech is often headed 'Ar'nt or Ain't I a woman' and quoted extensively, most scholars today are agreed that the original is more authentic. In it the admission of illiteracy is found but also a sophisticated biblical and logical argument from a woman who by now had considerable experience of speaking at anti-slavery and feminist meetings.[4]

The speaker, Isabella Baumfree, was born into slavery in Ulster County, New York, in the last years of the eighteenth century on the estate of a Dutch family, the Hardenburghs. In 1808 she was sold to an Englishman, and in 1810 she was again sold locally to John J. Dumont. Dumont gave the early appearance of being a more humane owner, partly because he valued her loyalty and devoted behaviour. However it was likely that he sexually violated her, and he certainly whipped her. A tall strong woman, she worked all hours in the house and the field, was married to Thomas and bore five children.[5]

Slavery in New York State was abolished in 1828. Dupont had promised to free her in 1827 but refused on the grounds of her disability leaving her tasks unfulfilled. After a few more months she

---

3. *The Anti-Slavery Bugle* (Oct. 1856).
4. Jean Fagan Yellin, *Harriet Jacobs, A Life* (Kansas: Basic Books, 2004). Yellin's research in papers at the University of Rochester and the North Carolina Archives led to a new edition of the *Incidents* in 1987.
5. The reminiscences of these early years until she settled in Northampton, MA, in 1843 are found in *Narrative of Sojourner Truth* transcribed by Olive Gilbert and first published by the author in 1850 in Boston. The page references are from an unabridged edition by Dover Publications, Mineola, NY, 1997.

left his farm in the early morning, taking her infant daughter with her, and sought help with a sympathetic family, the Van Wagenens. Dumont demanded her return, but Isaac Van Wagenen declaring his opposition to slavery, offered $25 to cover the remainder of Isabella's services for her and the child. Though still technically enslaved, she made landmark history as the first black woman in America to successfully sue through a County Court for the return of her son Peter who had been sold and resold illegally to Alabama.[6]

Isabella Baumfree went through a series of dramatic shifts in her understanding of the Christian faith. In her later memoirs she recalled how she believed that slavery was God's will, and that being obedient to the Dumonts was as important as being obedient to God, if not more so. When she began to renounce slavery and had liberated herself, she even returned to minister to the Dumonts in their old age. At an early age her mother, from whom she was separated and sold for $100 when she was 9 years old, had instructed her to call on God at all times of trouble. Isabella remembered that she was taught to say the Lord's Prayer in Dutch, to value obedience, honesty and truth, the latter being crucial in later life.

Her perception of God in slavery changed considerably over the years. Her mother's idea of God as 'a great man', 'high in the sky' and unapproachable, even though the subject of prayer petitions, fitted the rationale of the system so much that she compared God to a slave-'owner'. However when she moved from enslavement to free servanthood with the Van Wagenens, she developed enough spirit to question God in her prayers, and even to bargain with the divine. This led, she said, to a feeling of disinterest and forgetfulness of God. At that point she had a vision of God's overwhelming judgement of her 'sinfulness' and she feared to approach God. A dramatic conversion then occurred. Isabella had heard people speak of Jesus, whom she thought was an eminent man akin to George Washington, but she had a burning conviction that she heard Jesus calling her and declaring his love for her. The fear of God as a 'consuming fire' disappeared, although there was enough of raw Calvinist doctrine imbibed from her contacts with the Dutch to convince her of her utter 'vileness'.[7]

In 1829 she moved to New York City to undertake domestic service as a free woman. Shortly before leaving Ulster County, Isabella had

---

6. *Narrative*, pp. 18-20, 23-28.
7. Ibid., pp. 31-40.

been received into the Methodist Church, but in the city she became disillusioned with them, and transferred to the Zion African Church, the founder church of what later would be the worldwide African Methodist Episcopal Zion denomination. She became fascinated and influenced by the varieties of new Pentecostal and 'spirit filled' religious expressions, that emerged from 'The Great Awakening' in America. When working as housekeeper to a Presbyterian business man turned evangelist and religious fanatic, she became embroiled with the leader of an ill-fated movement, Robert Matthias. Matthias was an immensely corrupt and violent man. He founded what now would be called a sect, in which he ruled the members with an iron fist in what he called his residential 'Kingdom'. Possibly, as in her projected return to the Dumonts, Isabella sought in this community a place in a 'family, for all that Matthias beat her, as he did the others who challenged him, and refused to allow her to preach, something that she had done in her previous church'. Even after 1835, when he served a prison sentence for violence and illegal activities, Isabella felt attached to him, and wanted to follow him as he went west.[8]

However she did leave New York with the conviction that she was called to evangelise, and took the name Sojourner Truth for the rest of her life. This was highly significant. For all she craved settled family and communities, she saw herself always as one who journeyed. She was a free spirit who believed that she was a temporary inhabitant of a world which, as many religious groups thought, would soon end by the coming of Jesus. She had become disillusioned with the city, which she compared to Sodom and Gomorrah in the Bible. Her hatred of falsehood within the institution of slavery and her experience of the Matthias community meant that she valued unswerving devotion to truth, and yet her conviction that God was revealing divine purpose for her never plunged her into the trap of believing that all her actions were guaranteed to be righteous.

Another community to which she gravitated was the Northampton Association for Education and Industry in Massachusetts. This was founded by abolitionists and supported women's rights and religious toleration. It was a residential agricultural and manufacturing community, and Sojourner worked as a supervisor in the laundry. Significantly here she met William Lloyd Garrison and Frederick Douglass. Her preaching went hand in hand now with her strong

---

8. Ibid., pp. 50-56.

testimonies at anti-slavery meetings, and she found the beginnings of her passion for the rights of women. Truth also made a reputation for herself, not just by speaking, but in powerful rendering of hymns and songs. In the account of a camp meeting in 1844 where young hecklers spread themselves throughout the crowd, she admitted that she fled to a tent, fearing that as 'the only coloured person there' she would be attacked. Gathering courage, but failing to bring other leaders with her, she alone stood on a hill and sang a powerful hymn of the resurrection, which won them over until they urged her to preach, pray and sing.[9]

The Northampton Association went bankrupt and disbanded in 1846. The next year Truth went to work for George Bensen, a founder of the Association, and brother-in-law of Garrison. Four years later came the event for which she became best known, and where she combined anti-slavery with women's rights. In June 1851 she not only spoke at the Woman's Convention, but undertook an anti-slavery tour in company with William Lloyd Garrison and a visiting British Member of Parliament, George Thompson, a radical abolitionist. Truth described Thompson as 'genuine gentleman, the great hearted friend of my race'.[10] Throughout the 1850s she became deeply committed to the two causes, and also to the role that her new life marked for her – an itinerant preacher. Her height and commanding voice in prose or song made her a popular and controversial figure.

When the Civil War broke out she unreservedly supported Lincoln, and was confident that the Union side would bring about abolition. In the meantime Truth had become involved with a spiritualist group, and from 1857 she moved to a new progressive Christian community in Harmony, Michigan. Alongside women's suffrage, her passion in later life was for the employment and resettlement of formerly enslaved people, first in a village in Virginia, and later in the newly acquired lands of Kansas. Between 1870 and 1871 she collected signatories for a petition to Congress in 1874. Although it failed to achieve the settlement grants requested, in the next decade the backlash in the

---

9. Ibid., pp. 63-74 These are the last entries in *The Narrative*.
10. Nell Irvine Painter: *Sojourner Truth, A Life, A Symbol* (New York: Norton, 1996) pp. 258-87. Painter's book is based on research in University libraries in Princeton where she is a Professor Emeritus in History. She challenges many of the myths and stories about Sojourner Truth.

Southern states and the growth of the Ku Klux Klan, with its terror tactics, drove many freed blacks who feared a return to slavery to move to Kansas. Truth supported them by personal visits and speaking tours.[11]

Sojourner Truth's most recent biographer subtitled her work 'A life, a symbol'. This life became an iconic symbol for anti-slavery, women's suffrage and much else in the progressive field, and after her death in 1883 many memorials were erected to her. And yet, in spite of all that she did Sojourner Truth remains a much more complex character than the adulation of many who wrote and spoke about her allow. She made great play of her ordinariness, although she had a network of influential contacts, and she sought out the great, if not always the good, as allies in her causes. She was involved in many cooperative enterprises and organisations, but she was also a loner and she was always on the move. Her natural gravitation was to interracial work, peace and justice, and yet ironically the last great cause of her life, resettlement, was to be on land taken from native Americans in brutal colonial military campaigns. There were tales of the admiration for her expressed by Lincoln and Grant. She met both presidents and Andrew Jackson, but recent evidence shows that they hardly gave her the time of day, simply reluctantly signing her autograph book.[12]

The kaleidoscope of her religious experience, and the certainty that through it all she had a direct line to the Almighty, marked her out in the same mould as the Hebrew prophets, or even of John the Baptiser. In a sense she was 'a voice crying in the wilderness', albeit a very powerful and prophetic one. One of the stories told of her was that she sat listening to Fredrick Douglass declaring that he had lost faith that black American would ever get justice. Truth leant over and in a deep voice, heard all over the house, intoned 'Frederick, is God dead?'[13] The question was inscribed on her tombstone and at a memorial eulogy in Washington, Douglass summed up her life: 'Venerable for age, distinguished for insight into human nature, remarkable for independence and courageous self-assertion, devoted to the welfare

---

11. Ibid., p.117.
12. Ibid., pp. 207-08.
13. Harriet Beecher Stowe, 'Sojourner Truth: The Libyan Sibyl', *Atlantic Monthly* (Apr. 1863), p. 480.

of her race, she has been for the last forty years an object of respect and admiration to social reformers everywhere.'[14]

Harriet Tubman (1820/2-1913) –Moses of the Underground Railroad

Harriet Tubman was born Araminita Ross in enslavement in Dorchester County, Maryland, in the early 1820s. From an early ago she suffered continual beatings for failing to keep awake at night to stop a white baby in the household from crying. But it was an even worse assault that all but killed her, leaving her maimed for life, that, according to one account, changed her life and 'launched her career as a liberator'. Whilst working in the fields as a teenager she followed an enslaved man pursued by his overseer. The man was apprehended in the village store and Harriet was ordered to whip him. She not only refused, but blocked the way for the overseer to pursue the fugitive. The overseer threw an iron weight at her which severely impacted on her skull, causing lifelong damage . From then on she was determined to liberate herself, and the seeds of loathing of the institution, planted at an early ago, began to develop.[15]

In 1844 she married John Tubman, a free man, but already she had planned to leave the South, after discovering that the Brodess family by whom she was now 'owned' had cheated her mother and her siblings of freedom, though they were legally entitled to it from their birth. In September 1849 she left the family to make her way through Delaware and into Pennsylvania. Immediately a notice appeared in the local paper under the name of Eliza Ann Brodess, for the apprehension of 'Minty' 'about 27 years of age, of chestnut colour, fine looking and about 5 feet high' with a reward of $50 in the state and $100 outside of it.[16]

Immediately she arrived in Philadelphia she planned to rescue others from slavery, at first her siblings and their families. In a sense it was the worst possible time. A new Fugitive Slave Act passed in 1850 in

---

14. Francis Titus, *Narrative of Sojourner Truth* (1884 edition), Introduction, pp. 9-10.
15. Earl Conrad, *Harriet Tubman, Negro Soldier and Abolitionist*,(New York: International Publishers, 1942), pp. 5-8.
16. Catherine Clinton, *Harriet Tubman: The Road to Freedom* (New York: Little Brown, 2004), p. 34.

a Congress presided over by a weak President Millard Fillmore, who was desperate to compromise on Southern issues, provided draconian penalties on those who harboured any enslaved men or women who had escaped anywhere in the USA. A new licence was given to law agents and slave hunters in what many termed 'The Bloodhound Act'. Harriet had already established links with the Underground Railroad's network of guides and 'stations' or places of refuge on the journey through the North. Not only had she to 'guide' fugitives under cover of darkness through Maryland and Delaware, but she also must find routes to Canada, a safe refuge since the abolition of slavery in the British Empire in 1834. There are many stories of her quietly singing hymns when she had to travel in the day with two purposes – to act the part of a harmless old lady, and in some cases to send coded messages to those in hiding.

How many trips she made and how many she rescued has been a matter of dispute amongst her biographers. As with Sojourner Truth, myths and claims were made by those who wanted to lionise her. Estimates range between fifteen and nineteen trips and the numbers rescued probably around 300 over the next decade.[17] Harriet Tubman was unique in being the sole female 'conductor' on the Underground Railroad and the only one who ventured back into the South. She carried a pistol with her, and threatened to use it, not so much for her own self-defence (she believed that God's purpose for her meant that she might live or die), but to force any fearful recalcitrant fugitives to continue, and not risk the capture of the whole party.

A major disappointment to her was her failure to get her husband John to join her. In 1849 he had refused to leave with her and another attempt was made in 1851 to persuade him. It was one of her most dangerous trips into the very heart of the area from which she had escaped. But he never responded to her messages, and then she discovered that he had taken another wife. By 1857 most of the family were in Canada where she herself spent the summers, but that year she brought her elderly parents there. The family home in Maryland now faced increasing threats, because her father Ben, now a freedman, often hid enslaved people on the run there. Her parents were now too frail to travel on foot. Harriet therefore acquired a primitive wagon

---

17. Milton C. Sernett, *Harriet Tubman: Myth, Memory, and History* (Durham, NC: Duke University Press, 2007), p. 6.

and old horse which they perched on whilst she drove through the night the 80 miles to the border.[18]

It has been claimed that Harriet Tubman's religious awakening emerged at the time that she sought her own freedom, and had the conviction that God was calling her to be an active liberator.[19] So certain of this was she that she sang a farewell 'spiritual' once as she passed her owner, ostensibly on an errand:

> I'll meet you in the morning
> I'm bound for the Promised Land
> On the other side of Jordan
> Bound for the Promised Land[20]

Harriet Tubman transferred this certainty of her divine mission to many whose liberty she facilitated. William Wells Brown, formerly enslaved, and by the 1850s a noted anti-slavery lecturer, told of a man he met in Canada who had been rescued from slavery and declared: 'The whites cant catch Moses (as she had been termed) 'cause she's born with the charm. The Lord has given Moses the power.'[21]

By 1858 Harriet Tubman's exploits had become legendary and it was then that the man whose martyrdom became a famous marching song of the Union Army song – John Brown from Kansas – met her in Canada. They immediately struck up a bond, and having failed to gain allies in men like William Lloyd Garrison and Frederick Douglass, Brown immediately sought Tubman as a key player in his armed struggle to overthrow slavery. On meeting her he is reputed to have shaken her hand three times saying, 'the First I see is General Tubman, the second is General Tubman, and the third is General Tubman'.[22] Tubman, who was now living half the year in St Catherines, just over the Canadian border, offered to recruit soldiers from those she had rescued, and to raise money. She might have been part of the uprising,

---

18. Clinton, *Harriet Tubman*, pp. 82-83, 113-14. Bradford, *Moses of her People*, p. 87.
19. Clinton, *Harriet Tubman*, p. 32.
20. Bradford, *Moses of her People*, p. 18-19.
21. W.W. Brown, *The Rising Sun or Antecedents on Advancement of the Colored Race* (Boston, 1874), p. 538.
22. Lillie B. Chase Wyman, 'The Story of Harriet Tubman', *New England Magazine* vol.14, (1896).

but took ill before the disastrous events at Harpers Ferry, Virginia. Like many she saw Brown as a martyr, and his death, about which she had a vision, as a divine sign that liberation was at hand.[23]

She had to wait another four years before that prospect appeared to be possible. Harriet Tubman made her last trip in the service of the Underground Railroad in the winter of 1860. By the following year the Civil War had broken out, and a number had fled the plantations to join the Union forces now in the South. Tubman had little faith in Lincoln, who seemed hesitant to employ black soldiers, and hoped to win over the border states. She used her contacts to gain entry into government service, although she was only many years later financially recognised for this. The Northern military recognised her potential usefulness based on her past rescue techniques, and from 1862 she was sent to the Carolinas as part spy, part first aider and part organiser and social worker for newly liberated men and woman in the areas held by the Union army.

One of the most iconic images of her which appeared in many biographical sketches was of this simply dressed slight woman holding a rifle as if she was holding a broom that reached almost to her shoulders. By 1863 the Union government policy was to weaken the South by actively facilitating the liberation of plantation slaves. With 300 'negro' troops, Tubman set out in 1863 with a navy night-time raid along the 50-mile Combahee river in South Carolina. Under her joint command with Colonel James Montgomery, an expert in guerrilla warfare, she directed an operation that lifted Confederate torpedoes in the river, set fire to plantations, and led to the rescue of enslaved men, women and children. She was the first woman ever to lead a government military campaign and gained huge respect even from Union officers from then on.[24]

In 1859 Harriet Tubman moved her elderly parents from the winters of Canada to the outskirts of Auburn, New York, where she had bought land from Senator William Seward, an abolitionist supporter. After the Civil War she returned there, and following her husband's murder in 1867, she married Nelson Davis, a former soldier 20 years her younger who was to die in 1888. The wedding was in Auburn Central Presbyterian Church in New York State in 1869. In the meantime she worked hard to secure accommodation and

---

23. Clinton, *Harriet Tubman,* pp. 128-36.
24. Conrad, *Harriet Tubman*, pp. 37-39.

employment for those who had been liberated. In 1897 she received a gift of a silk and linen shawl from Queen Victoria and her last photograph shows her wearing it.

By the time of Harriet Tubman's death in 1914 very few of those who had been her companions in the struggle were still alive. But two earlier comments reflect her legacy. One is by Frederick Douglass, responding to her request for a commendation in the forthcoming biography of her by Sarah Bradford in 1868. He wrote to Harriet:

> You ask for what you do not need, when you call on me for a letter of commendation. I need such words from you far more than you can need them for me, especially when your superior labours and devotion to the cause of the lately enslaved of our land are known as I have known them. What you have done has been witnessed by a few trembling, scarred and foot-sore bondmen and women, who you have led out of the house of bondage, and whose heartfelt 'God bless you' has been your only reward. I know of no one who has more willingly encountered more perils and hardships to serve our enslaved people than you have. It is to me a great pleasure and privilege to bear testimony for your character and works.[25]

William Still, director for years of the key office of the Underground Railroad in Philadelphia, wrote of her in 1895:

> Harriet Tubman had been their 'Moses.' She had faithfully gone down into Egypt, and delivered these bondsmen by her own heroism. Harriet was a woman of no pretensions, indeed, a more ordinary specimen of humanity could hardly be found amongst the most unfortunate-looking farmhands of the South. Yet in point of courage, shrewdness, and disinterested exertions to rescue her fellow-men [sic], by making personal visits to Maryland among the slaves, she was without her equal.[26]

---

25. Frederick Douglass to Harriet Tubman, 29 Aug. 1868.
26. William Still, *The Underground Railroad* (Philadelphia: Porter & Coates, revised ed. 1878), p. 295.

Harriet Tubman and Sojourner Truth met only once, in Boston in 1864, but they would have known of each other through many mutual contacts in the movement. Both would have taken part in many anti-slavery gatherings, though as one contemporary account stated, Truth would have been more likely to be on the platform, whilst Tubman would have been in the crowd. Although separated by nearly a generation in their ages, they shared much in common. Their early experience of the horrors of slavery, its extreme physical abuse and demands, the dehumanising fracturing of families at the auction block and the pressures to accept servitude, could have broken either of them. Instead, and without the benefits of literacy, they rose above it and undertook their great crusades with a steely determination and an equally strong faith, however expressed, in the certainty that God was with them all the way.

Chapter 9

Black Presbyterians in Cooperation and Conflict

While sir, slavery cuts off the colored portion of the community from religious principles, men are made infidels. What, they demand, is your Christianity? How do you regard your brethren? How do you treat them at the Lord's table? Where I traversing the ocean to circulate the Bible everywhere, while you frown upon them at the door ... Blessed be God that there is a war waging with slavery, that the granite rock is about to be rolled from its base. But as long as the colored man is to be looked on as an inferior caste, so long will they disregard his cries, his groans, his shrieks.
—Revd Theodore S. Wright, Speech to the New York State Anti-Slavery Society, 20 Sept. 1837

Brethren, it is as wrong for your lordly oppressors to keep you in slavery as it was for the man thief to steal our ancestors from the coast of Africa. You should therefore now use the same manner of resistance, as would have been just in our ancestors when the bloody foot-prints of the first remorseless soul-thief was placed upon the shores of our fatherland. The humblest peasant is as free in the sight of God as the proudest monarch that ever swayed a sceptre. Liberty is a spirit sent out from God, and like its great Author, is no respecter of persons
—Revd Henry Highland Garnet, 'Address to the Slaves of the United States of America', 1843

I now returned with all my renewed powers to the great theme – slavery It seemed now as I looked at it, to be more hideous than ever. I saw it now as an evil under God – as a sin not only against man, but also against God. The great and engrossing thought with me was, how shall I now employ my time and talents so to tell most effectively upon this system of wrong!

—Revd James W.C. Pennington,
The Fugitive Blacksmith (London, 1849)

Abolitionist Splits

It is one of the cruel ironies of history that movements that seek to change the world and right its wrongs all too often get so enmeshed in bitter disputes over methodology, and hand unwarranted victories to those who want to block change. The anti-slavery campaign in America was no exception. As we have seen, the Garrisonians in their American Anti-Slavery Society were totally opposed to the plans of the American Colonisation Society. That would be true of most abolitionists, black and white, although emigration, especially to places such as Haiti, now free of slavery, and Jamaica after 1834, seemed to be attractive to some. Another issue that separated those who joined the American and Foreign Anti-Slavery Society was that of relationship with religious bodies. Although there were some church leaders in his movement, William Lloyd Garrison had lost patience with the position of most denominations that, in his view, compromised with slavery, and allowed 'slave-owners' to remain in membership. He was not enamoured with political parties, even though he relied on some politicians for support. But he felt, with some justification, that the American Constitution and its high ideals had been indelibly besmirched by its acceptance of slavery, and could not be redeemed.

Yet it would be wrong to see the white abolitionist brothers Arthur and Lewis Tappan who broke with Garrison in 1841 and Founded the American and Foreign Anti-Slavery Society as being simply conservative and cautious[1]. Their exclusion of those who did not

---

1. Arthur Tappen (1786-1863) and Lewis (1788-1873) were former Unitarians who became Evangelicals. Lewis was instrumentally involved in supporting Africans who took refuge from the slave ship Amistad in 1841 through a successful case for freedom won in the US Supreme Court that year.

espouse a particular religious basis for anti-slavery activity, and even more their unwillingness, on supposed biblical grounds, to admit women to their ranks, certainly gave this impression. But such labels could not be conveniently pinned on them, not least because of the support given to their organisation by prominent Northern African American leaders as these emerged in the mid-nineteenth century, and the decades up to the time of emancipation. What had been a substantially white leadership before that time was to be challenged by some formidable formerly enslaved leaders who, driven by their faith, and often influenced by Reformation principles, in their oratory and their writing, and above all for their passion for education as a way to freedom, took the cause of emancipation into a different phase.

Frederick Douglass (1818-1895)

By far the best known black abolitionist leader in the nineteenth century was Frederick Douglass, who first liberated himself from the border state of Maryland in 1838 dressed as a sailor in Baltimore, where he had been hired out to work in the shipyards. His mainly self-education and his oratorical skills enabled him to become a much-sought-after speaker in the abolitionist cause. After assisting William Lloyd Garrison on *The Liberator,* with whom he split over the issue of political involvement – Garrison saw the political system as a dead end in the abolitionist cause – Douglass was later to found his own newspaper *The North Star,* and his three biographies were best-sellers. Although he claimed not to be interested in the rivalries that beset the American anti-slavery movement and used to say: 'I will speak at any meeting when freedom of speech is allowed and where I may do anything to expose the bloody system of slavery', he could be harsh in opposition to others in the cause, and his setting up of his own paper, with its selected correspondence was seen by some as a negation of this statement.[2]

During the Civil War, Douglass was an enthusiastic supporter of enslaved and free black recruits for the Union army, pressing President Lincoln for equal rights. In 1878 he became a Federal Marshall for the

---

2. A. Pettinger, *Frederick Douglass and Scotland 1846: Living an Anti-Slavery Life* (Edinburgh: Edinburgh University Press, 2019).

District of Columbia and between 1888 and 1991 served as American Consul-General to the Republic of Haiti.[3]

The Reformed tradition influenced and shaped a number of black abolitionist leaders. Although Douglass had no formal link with a Presbyterian or Congregational church, his first wedding was conducted by a Presbyterian Minister, James Pennington, who spanned both denominations, but his allegiance to the institutional national churches was loose, and he tended to throw in his lot with the growing black denominations.

Nevertheless, Frederick Douglass strode magisterially across the abolition movement with contacts with almost every leading anti-slavery campaigner, black and white, male and female. Amongst these were three outstanding African American Presbyterian ministers – Theodore S. Wright, Henry Highland Garnet and James W.C. Pennington – all powerful voices who often held and acted on very different convictions on some of the issues that were vital to the common goal of ending slavery. These included participation in the political process, commitment to violent rebellion, the place of women in the movement and cooperation with churches that had slaveholders in their membership. Sometimes the difference led to bitter conflict.

Theodore Sedgewick Wright (1797-1847)

Wright's[4] name is rarely found amongst the prominent nineteenth-century abolitionists, but he was a pioneer in personal achievement, educational zeal and organisation, and he inspired many who achieved much greater recognition. Born in Rhode Island to free parents who moved to New York, he attended the African Free School there before becoming in 1829 the first African American to graduate in theology from Princeton's Theological Seminary. Four years later Wright was to be the second pastor at First Colored Presbyterian Church in New York, which he served as senior minister from 1831 until 1847, the date when it became Shiloh Church in what is now Greenwich Village. Under

---

3. F. Douglass, *Narrative of the Life of Frederick Douglass, written by himself* (1845), *My Bondage and my Freedom* (1855), *Life and Times of Frederick Douglass* (1881).
4. Wright's unusual middle name was given to him in honour of a distinguished Massachusetts lawyer who defended an enslaved woman, which action effectively abolished slavery in that state.

his ministry in Shiloh it became a key 'station' in the Underground Railroad for over three decades, as was his house, 235 West Broadway.[5]

Although Wright had not himself suffered the harsh cruelty of personal slavery, he certainly experienced vicious racist attacks and the humiliation of discrimination throughout his life. One of the most notorious examples was when, attending a lecture in 1836 as an alumnus of Princeton, he was physically assaulted in the chapel by a 19 year-old student Thomas Ancrum, from South Carolina, with the words 'Out with the nigger. Don't let me see you here again.' The Seminary did nothing about this, but it was a turning point for Wright, who in his speeches and sermons affirmed the need for racial equality to be achieved before slavery could be destroyed.[6]

Wright's speech to the New York State Anti-Slavery Society in September 1837 'Prejudice Against the Colored Man', was a direct result of his Princeton experience. He admitted that he and his family were able to move freely, worship where they chose and enjoy domestic comfort. But he continued in support of a resolution against racial prejudice by claiming: 'We are still slaves – everywhere we feel the chain galling. It is by that prejudice which this resolution condemns, the spirit of slavery, which treats moral agents different from the rule of God, which treats them irrespective of their morals or intellectual cultivation.'

In his contention that racial prejudice 'withers hope' and 'destroys souls' Wright continued to place such treatment and racial segregation in opposition to the will of God, as in the excerpt at the start of this chapter. He ended by giving thanks for the anti-slavery movement which he had no wish to criticise, and he deemed the day that he joined the Society to be 'one of the proudest days of my life'.[7]

Theodore Wright was an enthusiast for mass gatherings to promote equality. He was actively involved in the National Conventions for Colored Citizens. These were wider ranging in their concern for arts, practical skills and leisure activities, but central to them was the issue of slavery and racial injustice. Wright at first supported a policy of non-resistance, but at the 1837 Convention he opposed a resolution

---

5. *American National Biography*, Vol. 24, p. 62.
6. Joseph Yaniellii, *White Supremacy at the Commencement of 1836* (Birmingham: Aston University, 2017).
7. Theodore S. Wright, 'Prejudice Against the Colored Man'. Speech to the New York State Anti-Slavery Society, Utica, 20 Sept. 1837.

that declared black self-defence as un-Christian. Six years later at the Convention he supported a call for rebellion by Henry Highland Garnet, a fellow founder of the breakaway American and Foreign Anti-Slavery Society.

Wright did not confine his passionate speeches to those of his own race who might be sympathetic. He was reputed not only to preach to 'slave-owners' who visited his church when they were in New York, but also to pray for their souls and to engage them in dialogue. He believed strongly in the principles of American democracy, and had faith that these would be implemented when American people were alerted to the injustices of slavery and discrimination. He died at the age of 50 in the full prime of his ministry, and his dream, over seventeen decades later, has still to be achieved.

Wright's faith in the American Constitution and the political process was one thing led him into conflict with William Lloyd Garrison. Garrison grudgingly acknowledged Wright's ministry and 'devotional spirit' in obituaries for him, but termed his willingness to work with any who were ready to take even a small step towards anti-slavery as 'betrayal'. Garrison was also a pacifist, and strongly objected to Wright's eventual support in 1843 for an uprising of enslaved people, as he did to the latter's support for the exclusion of women in anti-slavery activity. Although Wright did shift his position on some aspects, Garrison all too easy cut off contact with those who disagreed with him. Others who wrote much later concluded that Wright was a rare combination of uncompromising principle and firm commitment to radical, even revolutionary, political action, with a willingness also to use persuasion and appeal even to his opponents.[8]

Wright was always fiercely loyal to the Presbyterian Church, whose willingness to accommodate 'slave-owners' as members sorely tested him. At his death membership of his own congregation in New York stood at 413, making it the second largest African American church in the city. His funeral procession was huge. But perhaps the greatest measure of his standing in the Presbyterian Church was that in a mainly white Presbytery, he was elected Moderator at the age of 48.[9]

---

8. Bella Gross, 'Life and Times of Theodore S. Wright 1797-1847', *Negro History Bulletin* (June 1940).
9. Daniel Paul Morrison, 'Theodore Sedgewick Wright: African American Pioneer at Princeton Seminary, Prior to Emancipation'. Paper given at Princeton, 2 Dec.2016.

Henry Highland Garnet (1815-1882)

Garnet grew up in New York. having come out of slavery in Maryland as a child along with his parents and ten siblings, after attending a funeral in a covered wagon. He was schooled in New York, and later graduated from Oneida Theological College in the city, one of the few to admit students of all races. Further studies in theology were accompanied by his becoming a founder member of the American Anti-Slavery Society and graduating in 1838 from Onieda Theological Institute, in Whitesboro, New York, which also admitted all races. Garnet had three pastorates. From 1841-8 he was minister of Liberty Street Presbyterian Church in Troy, New York State, and from 1855 for nine years he served as pastor of the Shiloh Church, succeeding Theodore Wright. In 1864 he went to Washington to be minister of the Fifteenth Presbyterian Church, returning to serve again in Shiloh in 1870.

In between these years he spent two years and a half years in Britain at the invitation of the Free Produce Movement there, lecturing and advocating a boycott of products of slave labour, and served as a missionary in Jamaica for three years before health problems forced him to return to the United States in 1855. Garnet was the first African American to preach to the House of Representatives, which he did on 12 February 1865, focussing on the ending of slavery. It was always his wish to visit Africa. He was appointed US Minister to Liberia in West Africa in 1881, but died just months after his arrival in Monrovia.[10]

Henry Highland Garnet did not hold back in making his views known. Amongst those were his fervent support for voluntary emigration to Africa, to the West Indies or Mexico – he was founder of the African Civilisation Society that sought to establish a colony in Yoruba (Nigeria). With others he had the idea of even establishing black 'colonies' in the United States, but that idea, for obvious reasons, never got off the ground. He supported the Liberty Party, that later was incorporated into the Republican Party.[11] His most striking speech was his 1843 Call to Rebellion delivered in August 1841 before the

---

10. *American National Biography,* Vol. 24. p. 62.
11. Joel Schor, *Henry Highland Garnet: A Voice of Black Radicalism in the Nineteenth Century* (New York: Bloomsbury (1977). Martin.B Pasternak, Rise Now and Fly to Arms: The Life of Henry Highland Garnet', Ph.D. University of Massachusetts, Amherst, 1981.

National Negro Convention in Buffalo, New York. He was 27 years old at the time. It was, quite literally, a call to arms, addressed to 'the slaves of the United States'.

Garnet began by rehearsing the history of slavery since the early seventeenth century when so-called Christians exhibited to their forefathers: 'The worst features of corrupt and sordid hearts and convinced them that no cruelty is too great, and no robbery too abhorrent, for even enlightened men to perform, when influenced by avarice and lust.' Later, when slavery took root, he contended that as it 'had stretched its dark wings of death over the land', the church stood silently by. 'The priests prophesy falsely, and the people love to have it so,' he declared. And he pointed out that three millions of fellow-citizens were prohibited by the law of public opinion from reading 'The Book of Life' (the Bible).

It was, Garnet said, sinful for any to make voluntary submission to such degradation. The condition of slavery did not absolve the enslaved from moral obligation. So now, he argued, if a band of Christians enslaved a race of heathen men, keeping them 'in heathenism' and preventing them from becoming Christians, then would heaven not 'smile' on every effort which the injured might make to liberate themselves? The time had come for those in slavery to take up arms. He commended Denmark Vesey, Nat Turner and Joseph Cinque (the leader of a rebellion on the slave ship *Amistad*), and he ended with 'Let your motto be Resistance! Resistance! Resistance! Oppressed people have even secured their liberty without resistance. Brethren adieu! Trust in the living God! Labor for the peace of the human race. And remember that you are FOUR MILLIONS!'[12]

The call was accepted overwhelmingly with only seven votes against it. At first Theodore Wright was uneasy, but he declared himself in support. One of the dissenting voices was that of Frederick Douglass, and it led to a long-standing rift between him and Garnet. Both men had supported strong resolutions on the position of the churches which spoke of them as 'synagogues of Satan' and denied they were 'true churches of Christ' because of discriminatory practices and their connivance with slavery. But Douglass described the call for insurrection as having 'too much physical force both in the address and the last remarks'. He pled for the adoption of moral

---

12. Henry Highland Garnet, 'A Call to Rebellion'. Speech delivered at the National Negro Convention, Buffalo, NY, Aug. 1841.

force and claimed that if this message was heard by slaves it could lead to catastrophic insurrection.[13]

The conflict between Garnet and Douglass began at that Convention. Although Douglass himself was loyal to Garrison and the original Anti-Slavery Society in the 1850s and there was always a central tension in the positions of those who were involved in the two societies, one historian at least has argued that it was at base a rivalry between two powerful and equal leaders in intellect and oratory.[14]

If that was so, it was played out in a bitter, and at times petty, way over the issues of insurrection and colonisation. It also all too thinly hid the jealousy of each other's position in the abolitionist movement. In 1849 Douglas wrote to him 'the green-eyes monster has made you mad. Pardon me, when I tell you that you never imbibed a spirit so narrow from any dark son of our native Maryland, living or dead.' When Garnet returned to the United States from his spell in Jamaica and envisioned a group of African Americans supervising cotton crops, resisting the vestiges of the slave trade and spreading the Gospel, Douglas castigated him and his recruits as 'traitors' for leaving the United States. And when Douglass left for Britain after the failure of John Brown's uprising in 1859, Garnet taunted him with 'fleeing to be under the protection of the British lion'. Ironically by this time Douglass had abandoned his non-violent absolutism, but he declined to join Brown in the rebellion for pragmatic rather than moral reasons. Later during the Civil War he became much more sympathetic to emigration for African Americans.[15]

James William Charles Pennington (1807-1890)

James Pennington liberated himself from slavery in the border state of Maryland whilst still in his teens, having been trained as a carpenter and blacksmith.[16] After reaching Pennsylvania he was given employment and taught literacy by a Quaker couple, William

---

13. *Minutes of the National Convention of Coloured Citizens held at Buffalo, 15-19 August 1843* (New York: Piercy & Reid, 1843), pp. 13-19.
14. Joel Schor, 'The Rivalry between Frederick Douglass and Henry Highland Garnet', *Journal of Negro History,* Vol. 64, no. 1 (1979). pp. 30-38.
15. Ibid.
16. An account of Pennington's early life and self-liberation is found in his book *The Fugitive Blacksmith* (1849).

and Phobe Wright, and moved to New York in 1828, a state that had very recently abolished slavery. It was there that he became involved in the life of Shiloh Presbyterian Church under the direction of Revd Samuel Cox, who was to be an influence throughout his life and one who led him at times to change direction. Seeking a wider education, he applied to study theology at Yale, where he was only accepted if he sat at the back of the class and asked no questions. Graduation was out of the question (the first black student to receive a degree at Yale was in 1857) but Pennington was ordained in 1840, and ministered in various Presbyterian and Congregational churches in Connecticut, becoming the first black Moderator of the Hartford Central Association of Congregational Churches. In 1849 he was awarded an Hon DD by the University of Heidelburg in Germany, again breaking new ground for a still unfree person. In 2016, 160 years later, Yale recognised his achievements.[17]

Pennington spent time in the 1840s and early 1950s in Jamaica and in Britain and on his return in 1852, as his freedom had already been bought through abolitionists abroad, he was able safely to return to a prestigious charge in New York. From there he broke new ground in being elected as Moderator of the Third Presbytery of New York in 1853. This attracted much criticism towards him. He had been an early advocate of breaking fellowship with any churches that were not willing to cut ties with 'slave-owners' and slavery, so there were many who could not understand this seeming reverse. Although his mentor Dr Cox was seen to be an abolitionist, he publicly resisted any calls for exclusion of churches when he spoke on platforms in America and Europe, and this was possibly why Pennington followed this position. Eventually, however, the tension was too great, and in 1864 Pennington severed ties with the white-dominated Presbyterian Church and joined the Missouri Conference of the African Methodist Episcopal Church under whose auspices he was appointed to pastorates in Mississippi, Maine and Florida, where he died in 1870.

Pennington was deeply disappointed when in the 1840s the Black Convention was abolished. He felt that it was an essential tool towards advancing both the end of slavery and the training of black leadership. Education for him was fundamental, and he followed the Presbyterian reformers not only seeing it as a tool of liberation from

---

17. E.H. Thomas, *James W.L. Pennington: African American Churchman and Abolitionist* (Abingdon, Oxon: Routledge, 1995).

slavery, but for the future of all black advancement, and as essential to the evangelism of all of his race. He defined education as 'a process of intellect embodied in action' and saw intellect as providing 'those powers of the human soul, as distinct from mere instinct, which alone enable man to reason and reflect'.

This was shown in his own life. Amidst the burden of preaching, pastoral work, evangelism and administration, James Pennington was an active historian and writer. In the late 1830s and early 1840s he made frequent contributions to *The Colored American* and then founded and edited *The Clarksonian*. In 1850 he joined the growing number of those wrote about personal experience of enslavement and liberation in the publication of his memoir *The Fugitive Blacksmith*. Nine years previously he had compiled what many have cited as the first comprehensive history of African Americans, *A Text Book of the Origin and History of the Colored People* – an analysis of the evolution of race and blackness.

This was a history which sought to refute the false theories about black origins and the myth of innate inferiority, a 'justification' for slavery and enforced barriers to advancement. He challenged the 'theology' that interpreted Genesis and the 'curse' on Canaan that was passed down through generations, and refuted the identification of the black races with the descendants of Caanan, a theology accepted until the late mid-twentieth century by the white Netherlands Reformed Church in South Africa.[18]

James Pennington was an intriguing combination of radical and conservative views and actions all his life, alongside being a leading intellectual and activist. When he joined the Tappan brothers in their new Society, holding to the ban of the involvement of women in the movement, he held to a very strict moral code over against Garrison's liberalism and refusal to keep the abolition movement on the track of strict religious principles. He was the author of a stinging attack on Garrison, yet believed that he made 'meaningful efforts for the black race'.[19]

Pennington became involved in 1841 in the famous case of enslaved Africans who took over the ship *Amistad* which went to

---

18. J. Pennington, *A Text Book of the Origin and History etc, etc of Colored People* (Hartford, CT, 1841).
19. R.J.M. Blackett, *Beating Against the Barriers: The Lives of Six Nineteenth Century Afro-Americans* (Ithaca, NY: Cornell University Press, 1989), pp. 48-53, 63-70.

the Supreme Court, from which their freedom and return to Africa was achieved.[20] The Tappan brothers were deeply involved in this and although Pennington does not feature before the judgment his interest was in Americans to be appointed as missionaries to Africa and the Caribbean. In 1841 Union Missionary Society was largely his inspiration. It included several of the freed Mendians on the *Amistad* and Pennington acted as its President. Although he had been firmly opposed to schemes for black emigration to Canada several years previously and any other 'colonisation' schemes, he saw the possibilities now of black-led missionary enterprises to bring the Gospel to 'unbelieving tribes of men'. He sold land he owned in New Haven, tried to raise money from impoverished black communities and eventually split with Lewis Tappen who saw the UMS as a competitor with his own Mendian Committee.[21]

Much later he clarified his position on colonisation and mission. Africa had enough population and did not need emigrants. He argued that there must be a distinction between colonisation and Christianisation. Africa needs 'bibles, missionaries, well qualified teachers, and as many Christian families as can be spared to them, to go for the purpose of advancement of the missionary enterprise'.[22]

Pennington declared himself a pacifist and opposed any violence in resisting slavery, but when the Civil War broke he joined Frederick Douglass in assisting recruitment for the Union Army. Until the Draft Riots of 1863, when his wife was threatened with violence and many were murdered, he kept to his stance that violence was no answer in the struggle against slavery and racism but then he declared 'self defence is the first law of nature'. He left the white-dominated Presbyterian church and joined the AME Missouri Conference.[23]

It was perhaps because of these contradictions and conflicts that, despite being one of the outstanding black churchmen of his age, James Pennington had so many ups and downs in his talented life. At times he was without a charge. His married life seems to have been an enigma, and he struggled for a while with alcoholism, though by the time of his death he had that under control. He was certainly learned,

---

20. Howard Jones, *Mutiny on the Amistad* (Oxford: Oxford University Press, 1987).
21. Blackett, *Beating Against the Barriers*, pp. 8, 23-24.
22. Ibid., p. 55.
23. Ibid., pp. 80-81.

dedicated and this was his uncompromising analysis of the core of chattel slavery:

> The being of slavery, it's soul and it's body, lives and moves in the chattel principle, the property principle, the bill of sale principle; the cart-whip, starvation, and nakedness, are its inevitable consequences.. you cannot constitute slavery without the chattel principle and with the chattel principal you cannot save it from these results. Talk not about kind and Christian masters. They are not masters of the system. The system is master of them.[24]

Their Contribution to the Struggle

It goes without saying that these three Presbyterian leaders held an abiding hatred of slavery and brought theological tools to seek its destruction. All held strong positions on the need to expunge slavery (and indeed racial disadvantage) from the church, but they were divided between each other and with other prominent abolitionists on the question of whether they could work, and accept leadership, within the structure that accommodated slavery. Although this and other factors in his relationship with the Presbyterian Church was too much in the end for Pennington. Wright and Garnet remained in a white-dominated church structure and they parted company both with Douglass, who, although still believing in working within official structures, rejected any cooperation with churches that allowed 'slave-owners' in their membership and indeed with the Garrisonians who had long since rejected the value of any such cooperation. This contrast was even more sharply seen in Wright's political embrace of the Liberty Party.

Although divisions in a cause inevitably weaken it, the above leaders were able, in spite of their differences, to effectively combine an overall passion for the liberating power of education with communication to a wider national and international audience in oratory or in writing (and sometimes both). They could sway audiences, especially when, in

---

24. Walter Johnson, *Soul by Soul: Life Among the Ante-Bellum Slave Market* (Cambridge, MA, 1999), p. 218, cited in D.B. Davis, *Inhuman Bondage: The Rise and Fall of Slavery in the New World* (Oxford: Oxford University Press, 2006), p. 193.

two cases, Garnet and Pennington, they undertook extensive overseas trips to promote the cause of abolition. They used their training and natural ability in the pulpit to drive the message through in no uncertain terms, although in their personal lives they had to struggle with many demons and dilemmas.

There is no doubt that, without any of them, the anti-slavery movement would have been impoverished, and the institution would have remained more complacent in the public mind. Although it took a bitter war to destroy it, and the legacy is still to be redeemed today, men of faith such as these were able to give practical support to so many who sought to liberate themselves from chains in ways that may not have been immediately apparent, but has recently been recognised by a new generation of historians, who have given more credence to the labours of leading black churchmen.

Chapter 10

Visiting the Reformation Roots

Eighteenth Century Scotland is an extraordinary case of a small society that developed a heavy economic commitment to slavery at the very time when its intelligentsia were vehemently criticising it.
—C. Duncan Rice[1]

The free hills of old Scotland, where the ancient 'Black Douglass' once met his foes ... almost every hill, river, mountain and lake of which has been made classic by the heroic deeds of her noble sons. Scarcely a stream but has been poured into song, or a hill that has been associated with some fierce and bloody conflict between liberty and slavery.
—Frederick Douglass to Francis Jackson, 29 Jan. 1846

Scotland the Brave?

Duncan Rice's comment ably sums up the fact that Scotland was disproportionally involved in chattel slavery in the eighteenth and early nineteenth century. The Clearances from the land of whole rural communities where the more profitable sheep replaced tenant farmers resulted, as we have seen, in many of the dispossessed settling in the New World, if they survived the transatlantic journey. Scotland was

---

1. Rice, *The Scots Abolitionists*, p. 19.

also a land, as has only been recognised recently, whose industrial revolution was fuelled considerably by the labour of those who were enslaved overseas. Glasgow's commercial development since the early eighteenth century owed its capital to the proceeds of tobacco, sugar and cotton. Recent research on compensation claims after the abolition of slavery in the British Empire in 1834, showed not only that these amounted to the incredible figure at that time of £20 million, but that Scottish individual investors, funds sent home from the colonies and generous endowments for schools, churches, hospitals and many other public bodies all too often stemmed from the profits of slavery.[2]

Nevertheless there was another side of the equation. In the petitions to Parliament calling for the ending of the slave trade in 1788 and 1792 and those calling for a similar legal abolition of plantation slavery between 1823 and 1834, Scotland's total within Britain and Ireland was disproportionate for her population. Although there was opposition to this activity, not least for areas that had commercial interests in slavery, and caution over such a radical step, not one churchman in Scotland, in contrast to its southern neighbour, attempted a theological defence of the institution. In contrast many of the petitions came from courts of the churches in Scotland and universities, trades councils and other public bodies used theological attacks on the continuation of the slave trade and slavery and even warned of divine wrath on any nation that sustained this evil.[3]

Slavery was legally outlawed in Scotland in 1788 when in the third case of enslaved men that came before the land's highest judicial body, the Court of Session, a majority of judges ruled that Sir John Wedderburn, who had brought Joseph Knight as his servant from Jamaica to Perthshire, had no right to deny Knight his freedom. One of the judges, Lord Auchinleck, father of James Boswell, concluded his speech with the words 'Is a man a slave because he is black? I do not think so. He is our brother and he is a man. He is in the land of liberty: let him remain there.'[4]

---

2. T.M. Devine, 'Lost to History', in T.M. Devine (ed.), *Recovering Scotland's Slavery Past: The Caribbean Connection* (Edinburgh: Edinburgh University Press, 2015).
3. Whyte, *Scotland and the Abolition of Black Slavery*, pp. 99-101, 247.
4. *Caledonian Mercury*, 17 Jan. 1778. An excellently researched historical novel deals with this case – James Robertson, *Joseph Knight* (London: Forth Estate, 2003).

The Knight case was preceded by two earlier ones. The case which involved John Witherspoon's certificate that he gave to James Montgomery was before the Court of Session, but ceased with Montgomery's death. The second one was in Fife in 1790 and resulted in the newly baptised David Spens whose 'master' Dr Dalrymple intended send him back to Grenada to be sold, being freed on the sudden death of Dalrymple.

In all three cases lawyers on both sides argued part of the case on their interpretation of early Christian history and practice, making use of biblical passages that gave authority to their position. Nothing illustrated this better than attitudes to baptism. It had long been held, not least in England, let alone in the colonies, that Christian baptism did not confer physical, as well as spiritual, freedom. The justification sometimes offered for enslaving people in Africa was that they were 'heathen' and were being given the 'benefit' of a Christian upbringing and even salvation! There was very little attention given in English courts to this issue, although sometimes lawyers for the enslaved raised it.[5]

However Calvinist Scotland saw a very different pattern. In 1756 Lord Bankton, senior judge in the Montgomery case, stated that he could not rule on whether baptism conferred earthly freedom on an enslaved person. The fact that he considered it showed the place of theological considerations in eighteenth-century Scotland.[6] David Spens, assisted by three lawyers, in his 1770s submission to the Court of Session, affirmed that, though he was 'formerly an heathen slave' but now baptised into the Church of Christ 'where there is no vestige of slavery allowed' – a rather optimist judgement – he was 'now by that liberate and set free'. As indeed he was, since the master's death concluded the case.[7]

James McCune Smith (1813-1865)

James McCune Smith was not a visitor to Scotland, but a highly regarded participant in the Scottish abolition story during his time as a student in the University of Glasgow between 1832 and 1836.

---

5. Whyte, *Scotland and the Abolition of Black Slavery*, ch. 2, pp. 9-40.
6. Ibid.
7. A.S. Cunningham, *Rambles in the Parishes of Scoonie and Wemyss* (Leven, 1905), pp. 154-8. David W. Blight.

Until recently his name was hardly ever found in the references to black abolitionists – even his descendants knew little about him. He never wrote a book and his papers were never compiled as a collection until recently. Despite that, his speeches, letters and essays show a wide knowledge of philosophy, history, literature and theology.[8] In company with the others he was born in slavery. He saw little of its harshest features, but enough to fuel his passionate hatred of it and his determination to use his talents to further its eradication.

McCune Smith was freed in 1827 when New York State passed an Emancipation Act. He graduated with honours from the African Free School in the state, but was denied medical training in New York's two medical schools because of his race. Through contacts made by a black Episcopalian minister, Peter Williams, he travelled to Scotland in 1832 and enrolled in the University of Glasgow's medical school, taking three degrees and returning to the United States in 1838 as the first professionally trained black physician in the country.[9]

While in Glasgow, McCune Smith was an active member of the Glasgow Emancipation Society, one of whose secretaries was William Smeal, a Quaker merchant whose relatives were actively involved in similar bodies in Edinburgh and Aberdeen. At the time there was a great deal of public outcry over the delay in abolishing slavery in the British Empire. The 1833 Act, shortly after McCune Smith's arrival, was hedged round with all kinds of compromises to appease the West Indian planters. One of these was that all who were 'freed' were required to stay and continue to work on the plantation for an unspecified time, which was later settled on as eight years. Observers noted that the conditions of those enslaved had scarcely altered, and in many cases their treatment had become even more harsh. The Glasgow Emancipation Society took a leading role in the early 1830s in the campaign to abolish the Apprenticeship Scheme, as it was termed.

In March 1836 James McCune Smith seconded a motion at the Society's Annual Meeting to agree to send a petition to the House of Commons calling for an end of the scheme. This was finally achieved in 1838. By that time McCune had returned to New York, but not

---

8. 'In Search of Learning, Liberty, and Self Definition: James McCune Smith and the Ordeal of the Ante-Bellum Black Intellectual', *Afro-Americans in New York Life and History*, Vol. 9. no 2 (July 1985), pp. 7-25.
9. *American National Biography*, Vol. 20, pp. 216-17.

without incident. The minute books of the GES record how on 4 May 1837 the captain of the American ship *Copernicus* which was bound for New York, refused to allow him to board for fear that white people would be offended by being asked to share the passage with a black man. William Smeal and John Murray of the GES protested strongly to the captain, expressing their contempt for American racial prejudice, and took steps to ensure that McCune Smith would not be refused again. On 15 June the Society sent him a letter of appreciation of all that he had done for the cause, begin

> From the Committee of the Glasgow Emancipation Society to James McCune Smith Esq.MD
> Dear Friend and Brother, When you are about to leave our shores, and return to your native country, we cannot deny ourselves the gratification of tendering you a formal testimony of our esteem, in addition to all the common evidences of affection and respect for you which it has our privilege to give, during our intercourse for several years past.[10]

The following evening a dinner was held in his honour in the Tontine Hotel in the city, a well-known anti-slavery meeting place, and McCune Smith afterwards was able to return home to New York.

McCune Smith not only had a distinguished medical career amongst African Americans, but was an active member of Garrison's American Anti-Slavery Society, believing that moral persuasion was the best tool to achieve abolition peacefully. Later, however, under the influence of his friend Gerrit Smith, a wealthy white abolitionist, McCune Smith admitted the case for violent resistance. He was passionate about education and championed black suffrage, wrote history and medical books, and was active in highlighting and working against racial oppression and segregation in the North, both before and after the Civil War.

Frederick Douglass, for whose newspaper McCune Smith regularly wrote under the pseudonym 'Communipaw', reckoned that McCune Smith was the single most important influence in his life when he wrote:

---

10. *Minutes of the Glasgow Emancipation Society,* 1 Mar 1836, Smeal Collection, The Mitchell Library, Glasgow. Microfilm Reel 2.

> He was brave, so brave, that he knew how to esteem courage in others. Educated in Scotland, and breathing the free air of that country, he came back to his native land with, ideas of liberty which placed him in advance of most of his fellow citizens of African descent. He was not only a learned and skilful physician, but an effective speaker, and a keen and polished writer.[11]

Although a pioneer in medical journalism, McCune Smith was never admitted to the American Medical Association or even local medical bodies. Up until 2019 his time in Scotland was only recognised through a café off the High Street in Glasgow that bears his name. That year a new hub for international student learning was built and opened in the University of Glasgow in honour of him, made possible by the donations from other alumni all over the world.

Frederick Douglass in Scotland

Frederick Douglass in his writings both biographically and to friends back home, was an incurable romantic in his view of Scotland, not least because of the strong reception that he received in his first tour to assist the anti-slavery campaign movement in the country in 1846. At an early age he read the novels of Sir Walter Scott, himself a portrayer of a romantic and sanitised nation. Douglass, as the quotation at the start of this chapter indicates, bought into a version of Scotland which writers even at the end of that century were defining as a 'Kailyard' one.[12] But Douglass' love of Robert Burns' poems and songs was based on the common humanity to be found in them. He was possibly unaware at the time of the fact that the poet who wrote the poignant 'The Slave's Lament' was also planning to escape his debts (and possibly responsibilities to women) by setting

---

11. Douglass, *My Bondage and My Freedom*.
12. R.B. Cunninghame Graham was a politician, writer, landowner and poet whose colourful career in Scotland and South America spanned the late nineteenth and early twentieth centuries. In a recent biography Lachlan Munro shows how he despised the romantic view of Scotland's past and present which he dubbed 'Kailyard'. L. Munro, *R.B. Cunningham Graham.and Scotland: Party, Prose, and Political Aesthetics* (Edinburgh: Edinburgh University Press, 2022), pp. 139-76.

sail for Jamaica to work as a manager of enslaved men and women on the plantations there.[13]

Douglas made two visits to Scotland in 1846 and 1860 interspersed with journeys to England and Ireland. By far the most significant visit was the first one. He was invited by the Glasgow Emancipation Society which was concerned that the newly formed Free Church of Scotland had sought funds from Presbyterians in America, including congregations in the South, themselves supported by members engaged in plantation slavery. Abolitionists in both sides of the Atlantic were keen to challenge this, to see the money returned by the Free Church (a logistically impossible task) and to deny fellowship with any church which admitted slaveholders to communion as full members. When the Free Church delegation returned from America in 1844 a campaign was mounted to 'Send Back the Money'.[14]

Douglass arrived in Scotland in January 1846. Throughout that year he shared platforms with other American abolitionists, including William Lloyd Garrison. He was however the only black speaker, and in another letter to his friend Francis Jackson in Boston he reckoned that his colour was an advantage in his mission.[15] At every meeting he sought to gain sympathy for the enslaved by giving a graphic account of their lives and treatment. In the meantime the leadership of the Free Church maintained a defence of their position of hating slavery, but not accepting that they should break ties with American Presbyterians. The now elderly and sick leader Dr Thomas Chalmers spelt out their case in the Free Church journal *The Witness*, arguing that although slavery was a sin, there was a distinction between an institution and individual conduct. Chalmers also gave comforting assurances to his friend Thomas Smyth that he had no intention of breaking fellowship with him.[16]

---

13. In a recent book *Frederick Douglass and Scotland 1846: Living an Anti-Slavery Life* (Edinburgh: Edinburgh: University Press,2018) Alistair Pettinger suggests that Douglass's admiration for Burns was 'not unbounded' and that he skips over the poet's ambivalence on slavery to concentrate on his love of human rights.
14. Ibid. Whyte, '*Send Back the Money*',pp. 10-45; G. Shepperson 'The Free Church and American Slavery', *Scottish Historical Review*, Vol. 30 (Oct 1951).
15. 29 Jan 1846, cited in Pettinger, *Frederick Douglass and Scotland*, p. 209.
16. G. Shepperson, 'Notes and Documents: Thomas Chalmers, the Free Church of Scotland, and the South', *Journal of Southern History*, Vol. 30 (Oct. 1951). Whyte, '*Send Back the Money*', pp. 49-56.

From the start Douglass challenged the incompatibility of slaveholding or 'man-stealing' as he termed it, with Christianity. He contended that Christ has 'no concord with Beelzebub as the light can have no union with darkness'. In the east coast town of Arbroath he presented a full challenge to what he saw as a vacillation by Thomas Chalmers' distinction between the system and individuals. He affirmed agreement between himself and the Free Church that slavery was a sin, as was murder, adultery and theft, and he wondered if 'the Doctor' would denounce the robbery and murder involved in slaving but would not denounce the murderer or the robber. 'Oh the artful dodger,' he continued:

> A distinction ought to be made between sin and the sinner that, while slavery may be a heinous sin, the slaveholder may be a Christian, the representative of the blessed Saviour on earth, an heir of heaven and eternal glory, for such is what is implied by Christian fellowship. We have in one sentence that distinction should be made between the character of a system and the character of the persons whom circumstances have implicated therein... this doctrine carried out, does away with moral responsibility. All that a thief has to do is to plead that circumstances have implicated him in that theft, and he has Dr Chalmers to apologise for him and recognise him as a Christian.

In his final words Douglas pointed to a press report in New Orleans that slaveholders were very happy with Thomas Chalmers' position on slavery. By contrast he appealed to the people of Scotland to 'agitate' the question of holding Christian fellowship with slaveholders and to proclaim to the Free Church the need to 'Send Back the Money', confessing their wrongdoing. This, he said to great applause, would 'send slavery reeling towards its grave, as if struck by a bolt from heaven'.[17]

A clever tactic employed by Douglass was to focus on the issue of alcohol in addressing the various Temperance Societies, well supported by the churches in nineteenth-century Scotland, where alcoholism was causing so much social disruption. He would describe

---

17. J.W. Blessinghame (ed.), *The Frederick Douglass Papers: Speeches, Debates, and Interviews* (New Haven: Yale University Press, 1979) Vol 1, pp. 156-64, 12 Feb. 1846.

how the slaveholders would give alcoholic drink to enslaved people as a method of social control, particularly at weekends or festivals, where they had more free time. At a meeting in Glasgow he gave a graphic example of that:

> On a Saturday night it is quite common in the State of Maryland (the slave state from which I escaped) for masters to give their slaves a considerable quantity of whisky to keep them during the Sabbath in a state of stupidity At the time when they would be apt to devise means for their freedom- their masters give them of the stupefying draught, which paralyses their intellect and in this way prevents their emancipation.

In Paisley the next month Douglas expanded on this theme:

> In order to make a man a slave it is necessary to silence or drown his mind. It is not the flesh that objects to being bound – it is the spirit – it is the immortal mind which distinguishes man from the brute creation. To blind his affections it is necessary to befuddle his understanding. In no other way can this be accomplished as by using ardent spirits![18]

Douglass did not spare himself in the cause of the 'Send Back the Money' campaign. In one dramatic incident he climbed the Crags above the city of Edinburgh, armed with a spade, and accompanied by two women who he termed his 'fair Quakeresses', carved out in large letters 'Send Back the Money' on the grass, which was visible from the city below. When Baillie Gray of the City Council sent men up to apprehend him on a charge of felony, one of his female companions commented that a man who had faced the wrath of slaveholders would hardly quake at a threat from an Edinburgh Baillie.[19]

---

18. Ibid., p. 166, 18 Feb. 1846; p. 207, 30 Mar. 1846.
19. This incident was related by Revd John Campbell, a Scottish-born Congregational minister at a meeting to welcome Douglass at Finsbury Chapel, Moorfields, London on Friday 22 May 1846. The two Quakeresses were almost certainly Eliza and Jane Wigham, Edinburgh

Dramatic speeches and gestures led to Douglass featuring in some of the ballads and songs of this brief campaign. Not all of them were complimentary to him, but many were enthusiastically taken up by those who wanted a bit of light relief, and no doubt they had the silent approval of the national Church of Scotland and other foes of the Free Church. One parody had the claim: 'Douglass has blawn sic a flame, that we winna hae peace till that sillers sent hame'. Douglass, with some exaggeration, wrote to his friends home that the whole country was abuzz with anger about the Free Church's connivance with slavery.[20]

Yet there were other forces ranged against him. Although he did not suffer the crude attacks that he faced in Ireland, newspapers and individuals came near to it at times. *The Witness,* whilst giving full support to Thomas Chalmers' position, refrained from attacking Douglas, but wrote that year about 'arrows shot, not against American slaveholders but against the Free Church'. Others were not so diplomatic. In April 1846 the conservative *Scottish Guardian,* in a sneering editorial in which they referred to Douglass as 'the black', commented that if American slavery was abolished, 'Mr Douglass would instantly return to his more important duties as a chimney sweep.' Revd John Macnaughton of Paisley, in a pamphlet that year defending the Free Church position. termed Douglass an 'Ignorant runaway slave, who had picked up a few sentences which he was pleased to retail up and down the country'.[21]

By contrast William G. Allan, a contemporary African American professor in New York Central College, rated Douglass as unique in his oratorical powers. Allan wrote in *The Liberator* in 1852: 'he sways a magic wand. In the ability to imitate, he stands almost alone and unapproachable, and there is no actor living who would not give the world for such a face as his ... his slave-holders sermon is a masterpiece in its line.'[22]

The year 1846 was certainly Douglass' finest hour in Scotland. When he returned thirteen years later the 'Send Back the Money'

---

abolitionists and relatives of William Smeal, Secretary of the Glasgow Emancipation Society. Baillies in Scotland are senior Councillors.
20. Trans. 'Douglass has blown such a flame, that we will not have peace till that silver (money) is sent home'.
21. Whyte, *'Send Back the Money',* pp. 76, 78.
22. *The Liberator,* 29 Oct. 1852.

issue was well forgotten – the Free Church establishment had held firm and after the death of Thomas Chalmers in 1847 there was not an easy target for the opposition to aim at. The Glasgow Emancipation Society had been bankrupted by the cost of the campaign, and Scotland had moved on to other issues. Yet Douglass' work had prepared many Scots to receive other African Americans in exile who by the mid-century were once again able to receive shelter and to acquaint audiences with the reality of 'The Peculiar Institution'.

The Struggle continues but the Hosts are Divided

The trigger that brought many self-liberated enslaved men and women to Scotland (as to other parts of Britain) was the notorious Fugitive Slave Act which carried severe penalties for those who assisted them. In fact the 'success' of the legislation was very limited. Records show that by 1860 only 330 had been recaptured. The effective Underground Railroad managed to send a number to Britain. The Fugitive Slave Act was repealed in 1864 towards the end of the war.

Two who needed to evade capture and found their way to Scotland at this time were James Pennington and Henry Highland Garnet. The Free Produce Association in Britain, which had been active in attempts to get the public to boycott West Indian sugar in British slavery times, had now turned its attention on the need to encourage British people to refuse to buy products grown in slavery in America, as a means of assisting emancipation there. In 1849 Henry Highland Garnet agreed to be their agent on a tour of Britain, and before he arrived Pennington had agreed on his lecture tour of 1849–50 to prosecute the cause. Ten years previously Pennington had rather optimistically predicted that the day 'was hastening when we shall see a combination of all the great and generous powers of the earth against the bloody slave system by the proscription of slave produce'.[23]

Both Pennington and Garnet spoke about the advantages to all of trade in goods grown by the free, and by this time both were keen on Missionary work in the West Indies. Pennington had of course spent time in Jamaica. Garnet's opportunity came when he visited Scotland and met leading churchmen in the *United Presbyterian Church,* which had brought together those who rejected the established church, the Church of Scotland, and the Free Church. This led him

---

23. Blackett, *Beating Against the Barriers*, p. 47.

to be appointed a missionary to Jamaica, where he served from 1852 to 1855. The UP Church had anti-slavery credentials, especially in the 'Send Back the Money' campaign in the 1840s. The problem that the church faced in their station in Calabar, in today's Nigeria, was the discovery that the mission was accepting not only polygamists, but slaveholders, into its membership. Many of the membership of the Glasgow New Anti-Slavery Society, a new rival abolitionist body, included a number of United Presbyterian ministers and the issue was conveniently shelved.[24]

Pennington, Garnet and others when in Scotland were drawn into the divisions that were forming amongst anti-slavery activists there, partly, but by no means exclusively, as a result of the 'Send Back the Money' campaign. It has been suggested that these reflected the bitter divisions between the various branches of Presbyterianism; but they were also further complicated by the attachments made by visiting American abolitionists.[25] By 1850 the *Glasgow Emancipation Society*, whose sources of support had almost vanished, had not held a meeting for three years. In the meantime, despite his proclaimed willingness to work with anyone in the anti-slavery cause, Douglass' break with Garrison had taken place when he founded his own newspaper *The North Star* in the 1840s, and departed from the position of non-violence and non-cooperation with American institutions. In the meantime the Smeal family in Edinburgh, headed by the redoubtable Eliza and Jane Wigham, fared better in the Edinburgh Ladies Emancipation Society. They kept activity alive through the widespread support for the Boston Bazaar that supported Garrison. This was a means by which Scottish women were enabled to send goods from Scotland, often knitted clothes, to be sold in America to raise funds for *The Liberator*.

Pennington by late 1850 was already making a name for himself as a lecturer in Britain. He was sponsored in Scotland by the newly formed Glasgow Female Antislavery Society which, with its male counterpart, had recently been set up an alternative to the GES. Negotiations with lawyers over the estate of his former 'owner' had been taking place for some years and a plan had been agreed through a third party (Maryland law forbad direct manumission) to

---

24. Rice, *The Scots Abolitionists*, pp. 146-48.
25. Ibid. This emphasis is made throughout the book which underplays other factors.

purchase his freedom for $150. In the meantime supporters in Dunse, Berwickshire, had raised £125. Garrisonians questioned whether he had already had funds from Jamaica for this purpose, but this did not diminish the enthusiastic meeting where he was to receive his papers. He commented: 'I esteemed it amongst the finest events in my whole life that by your aid I have been delivered from this property principle of slavery.'[26]

Pennington's influence on the Scottish scene did not end with his return to America as a free man. There had been an attempt at reconciliation with the Glasgow Emancipation Society earlier in 1850 but this had failed, partly because of suspicions over his funding and his Heidelberg doctorate, but more because at that time he remained a minister in a denomination that accepted slaveholders in membership. The British and Foreign Anti-Slavery Society which had long-standing links with the Tappans' American one, supported the new Vigilance Committee in New York, which Pennington had established with the aim of supporting enslaved refugees from the Fugitive Slave Act, who were in the North without funds. This deepened the divisions in Glasgow.

At the beginning of 1851 William Smeal and the Glasgow Emancipation Society sprang to life again by organising a tour of Scotland by William Wells Brown and two others, William and Ellen Craft. Brown, who had liberated himself by 1833, was a veteran lecturer on slavery, had been in Britain for five years and had published his autobiography and an account of his travels in Europe. His two companions in the first three months of 1851 had a fascinating story. William and Ellen decided to free themselves from Macon, Georgia, at Christmas 1849, travelling under the disguise of William being the 'servant' of his light skinned wife, who posed as a sickly young white man needing treatment in Philadelphia, a haven for enslaved people who had liberated themselves. After a hair-raising journey by train and steamer when several times they could have been caught, they arrived in Philadelphia, and after some time were spirited to the safer city of Boston, where they settled. William established a cabinetmaking business and Ellen found employment in fine needlework. However the Fugitive Slave Act produced further

---

26. Blackett, *Beating Against the Barriers*, p. 5.

Visiting the Reformation Roots 137

threats and the Boston abolitionists sent them to Canada from where they sailed to Liverpool and journey on to Scotland.[27]

Scottish audiences were enraptured by their story. Meetings were held in the major cities and quite a few smaller towns. The pattern was to have Wells Brown speaking about the evils of American slavery and then inviting William Craft to tell the story of their journey. Then Ellen was presented to the audience who found it hard to appreciate that she had been in slavery. In press reports she was often reported as 'a white slave' and audiences, in a somewhat racist way, became more outraged at a light-skinned person having to endure the cruelty of slavery. The Crafts met a number of distinguished Scottish figures, including the phrenologist George Combe, in Edinburgh before moving to London for several years.[28]

If nothing else the public presence of those who could communicate the reality of American slavery kept the issue alive in Scotland for a while. The divisive nature of those years and the competition for funds between Douglass and Pennington's projects and that of the Garrisonians was not helpful for the cause in Scotland. Even Douglass' second tour in 1860 failed to rouse much in his audiences. In the meantime in 1853 the new female anti-slavery society invited the celebrated Mrs Harriet Beecher Stowe, author of *Uncle Tom's Cabin*, to tour Scotland. It was a divisive move. The Garrisonian loyalist Eliza Wigham characteristically described the tour as 'small anti-slavery', although she admired what the book had done to raise awareness in America.[29] The Stowe meetings were packed in a way that had not been seen for years but they appealed to the fashionable romanticism of middle- and upper-class Scots as opposed to the ordinary people who had often attended Douglass' rallies. Indeed the irony of this visit was the failure to make connections. Mrs Stowe was welcomed at Dunrobin Castle in Sutherland by the Duchess and went

---

27. This story was related by William Crafts when he published the story of his and Ellen's self-liberation. W. Craft, *Running a Thousand Miles for Freedom: The escape of Willian and Ellen Craft from Slavery* (London: William Tweedie, 1860).
28. W.W. Brown, *The American Fugitive in Europe: Sketches of Places and People Abroad* (Boston: Jewett & Co., 1855), pp. 200-01.
29. Rice, *The Scots Abolitionists,* p. 152.

on record as denying the truth of the authenticated record of one of the worse and most brutal of Clearances on the Sutherland estates.

Nothing perhaps illustrates the complex nature of anti-slavery in Scotland as the fact that when Civil War came there was considerable public sympathy for the South as the injured party and the underdog. The land of Burns and the popularity of human rights that led to such eighteenth-century support for enslaved people coming to Scotland and for petitions against slavery, was to see ships built in Scottish yards to enable the beleaguered Confederate States to smuggle goods past the Union blockades and to keep their cause alive for the time being. Perhaps nowhere are the ironies of history more evident than in the long story of the eventual bringing to an end of the 'Peculiar Institution' in the United States.[30]

---

30. E. Graham, *Clyde Built: Blockade Runners in the American Civil War* (Edinburgh: Birlinn, 2008).

Chapter 11

In the End of the Day

Professor Bernard Powers' judgement was that evangelism and Christian education produced more of an incentive for liberation from enslavement than a bond that persuaded enslaved people to remain obedient to their situation. This is powerfully reflected in the written accounts of the eighteenth and early nineteenth century, the verbal witness of elderly respondents to the research project in the 1930s, and in many documented sources in the increasing volume of literature on slavery in the early twenty-first century. Powers himself emphasised the importance of a wider window being offered to enslaved people by the Bible, both in the narrative of the Old Testament and the life and ministry of Jesus, reflecting a different world of possibility, not just after death, but in this life.

Jesus as Master

The acceptance of Jesus as Lord and Master over all people, basic to nineteenth-century Christianity, was a major Achilles' heel for the Peculiar Institution. In emphasising to earthly 'masters' their higher obligation to a heavenly one, as Thornwell and Jones did, the foundation was laid for the whole system to collapse, however unwilling these evangelists were to see that happen, at least in the short term. Genovese describes it in this way.

> No matter how obedient – however Uncle Tomish – Christianity made a slave, it also drove deep into his soul an

awareness of the moral limits of submission, for it placed a master above his own master and thereby dissolved the moral and ideological ground on which the very principle of absolute human lordship must rest. It was much more than malice that drove so many Southern masters to whip slaves for praying to God for this and that, and to demand that they address all grievances and wishes to their earthly masters.[1]

We have already seen instances of cruel reaction to prayers in the accounts of the formerly enslaved, and the need often to hold gatherings far from the earshot of the 'masters'. Plantation owners, or those whose preaching they often controlled, may have strongly emphasised the Pauline doctrine of submission to the powers that be, but as Genovese points out, the injunction from Jesus to render unto Caesar the things that are Caesar's, and to God the things that are God's, is 'deceptively two-edged'.[2] Alongside a call to submit, there was the recognition that humans have also an autonomy and a freedom over their own spiritual life. By arguing for that freedom, and establishing a limitation of power over people to the obligation of physical service, as men such as Thornwell did, meant that a system which was based on the masters' absolute control of mind as well as body, was challenged at its very roots.

Spirituals and Messages

Studies of the use of what until recently were referred to as 'negro spirituals' (the term was used by leaders such as Dr Martin Luther King in the Civil Rights era) show very clearly how terminology during times of slavery had many meanings in familiar songs. And ordinary woven materials, as well as enabling some warmth in the slave cabins, when hung outside often carried messages for those who undertook the hazardous journey to freedom.

Of course to display openly any obvious signs would be fatal, but white stereotypes of enslaved and free African Americans taking their relaxation by enjoying loud and uninhibited expressions in worship, and displaying intricately woven quilts, often masked very

---

1. Genovese, *Roll, Jordan, Roll*, p. 165.
2. Ibid.

different purposes for simple songs and decoration inside or outside their cabins.[3]

In recent times some have cast doubt on the theory that spirituals in the time of slavery not only brought comfort and strength, and reflected the feelings and longings of enslaved people, but also were used as coded signals in the bid for freedom. It is difficult to completely quantify this, but there is evidence that many were certainly used in this way. 'Steal Away, Steal Away, Steal Away to Jesus' is a prime example. As Harriet Tubman affirmed, it was her favourite to indicate to her potential charges that the time had come to move off.[4] Songs such as 'Wade in the Water', again sung by Tubman, with its reference to the river Jordan, were employed to indicate the importance of river crossings in enabling enslaved people to throw the bloodhounds, sent by many pursuers, off the scent. Once in the water it would be a more even contest – the pursuers would have to find a boat, especially if the night fugitives and their supporters had helped themselves to the only craft on the opposite side.

'Let us break bread together on our knees' with the addition, after three renderings of the first line, 'With our face to the rising sun' may not have been a coded signal for an immediate departure, but was certainly a reference to the promised land of Canada as the ultimate destination. One song, that encouraged those who heard it to expect more immediate instructions to prepare for a bid for freedom was 'Keep Your Lamps Trimmed and Burning'. This was a reference to Jesus' words to his disciples in the Parable of the Foolish Virgins to prepare for the coming of the Kingdom and not be taken unawares.[5] Preparation for the unknown, but opportune, time, was a key element necessary for liberation from slavery.

One of the most detailed, and most popular on the Underground Railroad, was 'Children Go Where I send you.' It, like many of that era, owed its inspiration to the journey of the children of Israel, in the biblical account in the book of Exodus. But it also incorporated the signs 'go one by one', 'two by two' sung in the open air, to indicate to

---

3. J.L. Tobin and R.G. Dobart, *Hidden in Plain View: A Secret Story of Quilts and the Underground Railroad* (New York: Doubleday, 1999).
4. Earl Conrad, 'Harriet Tubman: A Great Woman', *Negro Digest* (Aug. 1940).
5. Matthew 25:1-4.

the conductors on the Underground Railroad, the numbers that they should expect to arrive in the next 'station' or stage.

The best known known example in nineteenth-century literature was the liberation of Eliza in Harriet Beecher Stowe's *Uncle Tom's Cabin,* based on the area around Ripley, Ohio, where the abolitionist Presbyterian minister, Revd John Rankin, and his family used their house as a station on the Underground Railroad, sending signals over the river by a light shining in the top of their house or one nearer the river.[6]

Deception for Liberation

The ingenuity of those seeking their liberation was very well documented in publications after the American Civil War – to do so beforehand would have carried immense risks whilst the Fugitive Slave Act was in place. Individuals and groups of enslaved people used the power of biblically referenced phrases and songs to mask the real messages, and thus prevent white people from realising the threat to their institution until it was too late.

Deception and adaptation to a manner which satisfied whites was a technique of survival for enslaved and free African Americans, which was necessary during slavery and far beyond it. Yet repeated instruction by so many white preachers, codified in the writings of Charles Colcock Jones and James Henley Thornwell, that enslaved people who aspired to the Christian faith must never lie, cheat or use deception, not least to their 'masters', inevitably limited the armoury of the enslaved when seeking freedom.

When William Craft first spoke to audiences in Scotland in 1851 he confessed that, as a practising Christian, he felt guilty about the deception needed for their roles to be played out in their liberation. A response from a minister in the audience swiftly assured him that there was no question about that, even about the pretence, in the disguise necessary for his wife, to simulate a young and sickly white man. Any civilised person, he affirmed, would be sick to death with the evil system of slavery.[7] Nonetheless early training in truthful obedience left deep marks, even in the most fervent abolitionists during their

---

6. Ann Hagedorn, *Beyond the River: The Untold Story of the Heroes of the Underground Railroad* (New York: Simon & Schuster, 2002).
7. Meeting in Edinburgh's Nicolson Street Church, 30 Dec. 1850.

bids for freedom, as evidence in the cases of James Pennington and Sojourner Truth shows. In his autobiography Pennington had a section called 'The Great Moral Dilemma' in which he asked forgiveness of his readership for telling lies about having smallpox in order to scare his captors into releasing him.[8] All this would seem to support the theory advanced by some that, whereas in Roman and Greek times enslaved people were held by fear, Christianity imposed the unquestioning obedience of slaves to a moral duty. But the overwhelming evidence does not support this.

But just as deception in word, dress or manner was necessary to enable successful bids for freedom, so the entrenched Southern myths of enslaved people being accustomed to, if not contented with, their lot, and of white superior intelligence and benevolence, were some of the smokescreens that in fact assisted liberation. If as dedicated and able a person as Charles Colcock Jones was able to cling to part of that myth, and feel disappointed and betrayed by the disappearance of his 'servants' as the Northern armies reached Georgia, then this would be replicated so many times over amongst planters who had a fraction of his experience of the world outside their own society. Jesus' command to his disciples as noted in the Gospels, to be as 'wise as serpents and as harmless as doves', was a practice that was to be repeated endlessly in the attempts of enslaved people to seek their liberation.[9]

How many succeeded in that? One of the contemporary spirituals looking to a world without whips, overseers and splintered families was titled 'Many Thousand Gone'. Clearly there is much doubt about the numbers from border states such as North Carolina, Virginia, Kentucky and Maryland, let alone those further South. The United States Census of 1850 indicates that only just over a thousand liberated themselves that year, and in 1860 this figure was 800, but this needs to be questioned from two sides. The evidence given to Congress from the border states pressing urgently for the tighter legislation that became the Fugitive Slave Act in 1850 shows a claim of thousands of dollars 'worth' in the preceding years. Secondly, the success of the

---

8. Pennington, *The Fugitive Blacksmith*, pp. 216-17. Cited by Blackett in *Beating Against the Barriers,* p. 44. Blackett makes the point that Pennington is aiming at young readers and keen to impress on them the need for truthfulness.
9. Matthew 10:16.

Underground Railroad and the many stories told in later years witness to a far higher number, even if we allow for the obvious reluctance of the leaders and 'conductors' of the movement to keep records of those whose liberty they assisted. The most comprehensive local record was that made by Willian Still in Philadelphia, but his account, for obvious reasons, was not published until 1872.[10]

In the End of the Day– Enduring Faith

There is no doubt that the history of mainstream Christianity since the Constantine era has broadly been one of accommodation to the powers that be and to class and often racial classification. The imperial adoption of Christianity in AD 380 gave protection to what had previously been known sarcastically as 'the religion of slaves'. In its various divisions, East and West, it fell into the lure of power, with a hierarchical structure that belied its founder's example and instruction, and became over the centuries a formidable political empire. Modern historians have rightly emphasised the irony of how for centuries in Europe, and in the settlements overseas of those who left that Christian continent, the permanent enslavement of other human beings was accepted, and in many cases theologically justified.

Yet many historians underplay the way in which the Christian faith was always used to condemn such practice and to actively work for its destruction. It is not a narrative that is popular to acknowledge. Nevertheless in Europe as in America the great majority of those who campaigned against the institution were rooted in the Christian faith. It is of course true that they mainly undertook this from a privileged and safer position than those who risked all in seeking the destruction of their personal bonds and those of others.

Even less acknowledgement has been given to the fact that rebellions (often armed) were so often undertaken in the name of the one who was put to death as a criminal by imperial and religious powers that feared his revolutionary message. In that legacy stand not only the leaders of rebellions against enslavement in America, such as Daniel Vesey, Nat Turner and John Brown, but the many thousands

---

10. William Still, *The Underground Railroad, a Record of Facts, Authentic Narrative, Letters & C., Narrating Hardships, Hairbreadth Escapes and Death Struggles of the Slaves in their Efforts of Freedom* (Philadelphia, 1879).

of unnamed men and women who had the courage to resist and seek to destroy slavery, and even more remarkably, carried this same faith into the new lives that they forged for themselves on the other side of the barriers that divided bond from free.

Being devised by humans, the church structures which African Americans created for themselves in the face of considerable persecution were sometimes to carry, as we have seen, some of the marks of deep and bitter division. But this is outweighed by the miracle that so many of those who were denied freedom and humanity, even after emancipation, continued in their Christian faith, and bore witness in their spoken and written word to the liberating power of the Gospel in their lives that inspired them to break their chains. In this, those heroic men and women, most of whom are barely recognised in history, challenged and continue to do so today, the very nation that was founded on the supposed principles of physical and spiritual freedom, but which still in the twenty-first century has to deliver this reality for all of its citizens.

Index

Abolition of British Slavery 35
Act of Union Scotland/England 13
Address to the Public 60
Adger, Margaret 4, 7
Adger, Revd John 53, 58-59, 61, 73-74
African Colonisation Society 4
African Methodist Episcopal 41, 61, 101
American Anti-Slavery Society 111
American Colonisation Society 4, 62-63
American Revolution 19, 23, 31, 33, 37
Apartheid in South Africa 58
Apprenticeship Scheme 1830-1838 127
Auchinloch, Lord 125

Bain, John Mackintosh 14
Bankton, Lord 126
Baptism and Slavery 126
Beecher, Henry Ward 26
Beecher, Lynman 66
Bellinger, Edmund 51, 68
Benet, Governor Thomas 44, 48
Bensen, George 102
Bill of Rights 1776 33

Black, Joseph 34
Bowes, Margery 8
Brodess, Eliza Ann 104, 105
Brougham, Henry 15
Brown, John 25, 40, 106, 107, 118, 144
Brown, Revd Morris 41, 44
Brown, William Wells 83, 106, 136-137
Burns, Robert 15, 129, 138

Calvin, John 2, 6-12, 16-17, 32, 35, 69, 72, 78, 126
Carey, Lott 64
Chalmers, Dr.Thomas 10, 75-76, 130-131, 133-134
Charleston Churches 4, 41, 61, 73, 80
 Bethel Presbyterian 4
 Second Presbyterian 41, 61, 73, 80
 Ansen Street 61
 Emmanuel AME 41, 61
Charleston Courier 44
Church of Scotland 19, 22-23, 26, 40, 44, 52, 54, 73, 81, 83, 102, 107, 112, 118, 121, 128, 138, 142

Index

Civil War (USA) 5-6, 20, 23- 24, 26, 40, 44, 52, 54, 73, 81, 83, 102, 107, 112, 118, 121, 128, 138, 142
Clan System (Scotland) 57
Clarke, Prof Erskine 60, 69, 73
Clay, Henry 62
Colombia Seminary 3, 28, 30, 71, 77
Combe, George 137
Compensation Claims 1834 125
Confederate States 138
Confessions of Nat Turner 45
Constantine, Emperor 144
Cotton Boom 55
Court of Session 14
Covenanters 23, 25
Crafts, William and Ellen 136-137, 142
Criminalising Literacy 51
Cromwell, Oliver 11
Culloden, Battle of 13

Darien Petition 1739 14
Davies, Revd Samuel 28, 30
    Training for Ministry 28
    Funds for College of New Jersey 28
    'Apostle of the Enslaved' 29, 30
Davis, Prof David Brion 32, 69
Declaration of Independence 3, 30, 34
Douglas Frederick 48, 76, 83, 101, 103, 106, 108, 112-113, 117-118, 121-122, 124, 128-135, 137-138
    Liberated himself 112
    Dispute with Garrison 112
    Conflict with Garnet 118
    Romantic View of Scotland 129
    'Send Back the Money' 1846 130
    Conflict with Thomas Chalmers 131-132
    Temperance issues 132
    Songs, Action in Edinburgh, and Opposition to him 133

Dumont, John 99-101

Edward VI of England 8
Elizabeth, Queen of England 8, 9
Episcopalianism 23
Evangelical Allience 76
External Slave Trade 55

Filmore, President Millard 105
Finley, Robert 62
First Book of Discipline 6, 10, 11
Floyd, Governor 39
Ford, Prof Lacey K. 48, 56
Free Church of Scotland 22, 75, 76, 130, 131, 133, 134
Free Produce 116, 134

Garnet, Revd. Henry Highland 48, 110, 113, 115-118, 122, 128, 130, 134-136
    Education 116
    Free Produce Movement 116
    Africa Civilisation Society 116
    US Minister in Liberia 117
Garrison, William Lloyd 25, 50, 63, 97, 101, 102, 106, 111-112, 115, 118, 120, 130, 135-137
Genovese, Prof Eugene 54, 81, 89
George Thomson MP 102
Gerrit Smith 127
Glasgow Emancipation Society 135
'Godly Commonwealth' 11, 75, 117
Gordon, General 79
Grant, President 103
Gray Thomas 47
Green, Revd. Ashbet 21
Grimke, Emile 59
Grimke, Sarah 59
Grimke, Thomas 59

Haiti 41, 111, 113

Hamilton, James 44, 48
Hamilton, Patrick 7
Hammond, James Henry 51, 68
Hardenburgs 99
Harmony, Michigan 102
Henry, Revd Charles 53, 65
Hewat, Revd. Alexander 18, 19
Highland Clearances 13, 124, 138
Holt, Revd John 21
Harper William 51
Hopkins, Samuel 16, 17
Hume, David 15
Hutchison, Francis 32

Jacobite Cause 13, 31, 52
Jamaica 14, 15, 111, 116, 118, 119, 130
Jefferson, President Thomas 16, 62
Jesus of Nazareth, 2, 42, 59, 65, 70, 87, 89, 90, 96, 98-100, 101, 139, 140, 141, 143
Jones Revd Charles Colcock 69-73, 79, 138
   Inheriting Liberty Hall Plantation 6, 69
   Theological Teraing in the North 69
   Proposal to Synod on Religious Education 67, 68
   Savannah and Columbia Seminary 70-71
   Catachism 71-72
   Sale of enslaved woman 73
Jones, Prof Lawrence 28, 64

King Charles II 3, 23
King Dr Martin Luther 79, 140
Knight Case 1788 14, 126
Knox, John 2, 6, 7, 9, 11-12
   Family and Background 7
   Calvin and Geneva 8
   'Godly Commonwealth' 9, 11

Education Legacy 11, 12

Laurens, Martha 37
Laurens, Henry 34, 37
Laws on Mixing (Virginia) 51
Lenin, Vladimir 1
Liberty Party 116, 122
Lincoln, President Abraham 81, 102, 103, 107, 112
Locke, John 32
Long, Edward 15

Macaulay, Zachary 15, 17, 19, 97
Macleod, Revd Alexander 24, 25
Madison, President James 16, 62
Martin, Revd William 24
Mary of Guise 9
Mary, Queen of Scots 9
Matthias, Robert 101
McCune Smith, James 126-129
   Early Freedom 127
   To Scotland for Medical Studies 127
   Active in GES 127-128
   Denied passage back to USA 128
   Cooperation with Douglass 129
Methodist Church 41, 85, 101
Milligan, Revd A.A. 25
Moderate Party, Church of Scotland 19, 32
Monrovia, Liberia 62, 116
Montgomery v Sheddan Case 1756 31, 125
Moore, Thomas 45
Moray and Mar, Earl of 8
Moses, OT Prophet 43
Mott Lucretia 97
Munro, James, President 62
Murray, John 128

Nairn, Tom 6

Nelson, Revd. Isaac 76
North Star 112

Oglethorpe, Governor George 13, 14

Paisley St Georges Church 30
Paternalism 3, 53, 55-58
Peculiar Institution, the 3, 91, 134, 138
Pennington, Dr James 83, 86, 111, 113, 118, 119, 120, 121, 122, 123, 134, 136, 143
   The Fugitive Blacksmith 119
   Education Concern 119
   Heidelburg Degree 120
   The *Amistad* Case 120
   Conflicts and Pacifism 121-122
   Freedom purchased in Scotland 136
Pennsylvania Abolition of Slavery Society 79
Peters, Mr Albert 5
Petition to Congress 1874 102
Petitioning Campaign Scotland 1788-1824 25
Philadelphia, 34-36, 47, 49, 59, 74, 83, 108, 136, 143-144
Pope Pius IV 8, 9
Popular Party, Church of Scotland 19, 32
Powers, Professor Bernard 2, 139
Predestination 32, 58
Presbyterian Church USA 16, 20-23, 26-7, 61, 67-68, 81, 89, 117
   General Assembly 1818, 20-23, 26-27
   General Assembly 1845, 23
   General Assembly 1847, 89
   'Old School' Assembly 1845, 21
   Presbytery of New York 119
   Presbytery of South Carolina 61, 81
   Presbytery of Transylvania 20
   Synod of NY and Philadelphia 19
   Synod of N. Carolina 20
   Synod of Georgia and S. Carolina 67, 68
   Synod of South Carolina 23
Presbytery of the Confederacy 22
President Abraham Lincoln 81
Prioleau, Peter 42
Princeton 2, 17, 27, 28, 30, 33, 34, 69, 73, 113-114
Purcell, Jack, 'Gulla Jack' 42, 43, 44

Quamine, J. 17

Ramsay, David 27, 34-38
   Training and Education 36
   Influence of Rush 36
   Theory and Practice on Slavery 34, 35-38
Ramsay, Sabina 34
Rankin, Rev John 26, 142
Rebellion 39, 40-41, 43-45, 47-49, 54-55, 57-58, 61, 80, 90, 113, 115-118, 144, 148-49
Reformed Presbyterian Church 23, 25-26
Revolutionary War 16, 34, 54
Rhett, Robert 59
Rice, Prof C. Duncan 15, 124
Robertson, Principal William 19
Roman Catholic Church 3, 6-8
Roof, Dylan 61
Roper, Moses 82, 85, 86
Ross, Isaac 64
Rush, Benjamin 27, 34-36

Scots Confession of Faith 9, 10-11
Scottish 'Common Sense Realism' 77
Scottish Enlightenment 15, 77
Scottish Petitions on Slavery 15
Seabrook, Whitemarsh 49

Sermon on the Mount 24
Seward, William 107
Sharp , Granville 17, 37
Sheddan, Robert 30
Sierra Leone 17
Slave Trade Act 1819 62
Sloane, Revd J.R.W 25
Smeal William 127, 136
Smith, Adam 15
   Smyth, Revd Thomas 73-76, 81
   Belfast, Princeton, 2nd Presbyterian, 73
   The Unity of the Human Race 74
   Thomas Chalmers and the Free Church of Scotland 75, 76
   Civil War and Lincoln 51
Society of Friends (Quakers) 2, 16, 23
Songs of Liberation 141
South Carolina Legislature 34
Spanish Colonies 14
Spens v Dalrymple Case 1760 125
St Giles Cathedral, Edinburgh 9
Stephen, James 15
Still, William 109, 143
Stowe, Harriet Beecher 137
Sutherland, Duke and Duchess of 137-138

Tappan, Arthur 111
Tappan, Lewis 111
Tenant, Gilbert 28
Testimonies on Religion by several formerly Enslaved
   Clarke, Lewis and Milton 84, 88
   Wells Brown, William 85
   Northup Soloman 80, 86
   Jacobs, Harriet 88-89
   Moses, Andrew 89
   Cranberry, Mary Ellen 91

Hines Marriah, 91, 92, 94
Dawson, Anthony, 92
Sorrell, Ria, 92
Thomson, John 93
Bost, W.L. 94
The Great Awakening 27, 56
The Great Commission 59
The Liberator 24, 62, 97, 135
The Rights and Duty of Masters 78
The Southern Intelligencer 44
Thomson, George MP 102
Thornwell, Dr James Henley 67, 77, 78, 79, 80, 138
   Editor of *Presbyterian Review/ Southern Quarterly Review* 77
   Influences on him over slavery 78
   Rights and Duties of Masters 78
   Philosophy on Slavery 79
Tontine Hotel 128
Travis, Jo 46
Truth, Sojourner 96, 98-99, 100-103, 109
   'Aint I a woman' 98, 99
   Isabella Baumfree and her 'masters' 99, 100
   Perceptions of God and Slavery 100
   Call to Evangelism 101
   Northampton Association 101, 102
   Civil War and Lincoln 102, 103
   Tribute by Frederick Douglass 103
Tubman, Harriet 96, 104, 105, 106-109, 141
   Enslaved as Ardminita Rice 104
   Liberating herself and others 105
   Legendary Status in the Underground Railroad 106, 107
   Gift from Queen Victoria 108
   Tributes from Douglass and Still 109
Turner, Benjamin 47

Index

Turner, Nat 45, 49
   Visions and Reflections 45-46
   Rebellion and Death 47
   Questioning of his *Confessions* 47, 48

Uncle Tom's Cabin 82
Underground Railroad 25, 26, 106, 134
Union Army 107
United Presbyterian Church 134

Van Wagenen 100
Vassals and Serfs 78
Vesey, Denmark 39-40, 41-43, 50, 61, 144
   Capture and Enslavement 41
   Break with the Presbyerian Church 41
   Revolutionary Biblical Teaching 42-43

Walker, David 49
Ward Beecher, Henry 26
Washington President George 16
Wheatley Phyllis 16
Wilberforce William MP 19
Wilson, Leighton and Jane 6
Wright, Revd Theodore 110, 113, 114, 115, 116, 117, 119, 122
   Early education and pastorates 113
   1837 Speech 113-114
   Dispute with Garrison 115-117
   Loyalty to Presbyterian Church 15

Yamma, Bristol 17

Zechariah OT Prophet 42

You may also be interested in:

Send Back the Money!

The Free Church of Scotland and American Slavery

Iain Whyte

When the Free Church broke from the Church of Scotland in 1843 they sought money and support from inside and outside Scotland. A delegation which went to America in 1844 brought some money back gifted by sympathisers in the Southern slave states. A huge row broke out amongst abolitionists in Scotland and America and a campaign to 'Send Back the Money' was launched.

Iain Whyte's examination of the Free Church of Scotland's early involvement with American Presbyterianism reveals the ethical furore caused by a Church wishing to emancipate itself from the domination of a state-sanctioned established religion. The Free Church therefore found a ready affinity with those oppressed elsewhere, but subsequently found itself financially supported by the Southern slave states of America. Whyte sensitively handles this inherent contradiction in the political, ecclesiastical, and theological institutions, while informing the reader of the roles of charismatic characters such as Thomas Chalmers and Frederick Douglass, key individuals who did much to shape contemporary culture with action, great oratory, and rhetoric. The author adroitly draws parallels from the twentieth century onwards, leading the reader to a fuller and more nuanced understanding of the historic and topical issues within global Christianity, and the contentious topic of slavery.

Iain Whyte is the President of the Scottish Church History Society and an Honorary Post Doctoral Fellow at the Centre for Diaspora Studies, University of Edinburgh for his work in the history of slavery and abolition. He is the author of Scotland and the Abolition of Black Slavery 1756-1838.

Published 2012

Paperback ISBN: 978 0 227 17389 3
PDF ISBN: 978 0 227 90158 8
ePub ISBN: 978 0 227 90159 5

You may also be interested in:
The Bible, the Bullet, and the Ballot
Zimbabwe: The Impact of Christian Protest in Sociopolitical Transformation, ca. 1900-ca. 2000
Fabulous Moyo

The Bible, the Bullet, and the Ballot provides a balanced account of the role of Christians, Christian organisations, and churches in sociopolitical transformation over the bedrock of colonial and nationalist politics in the past century in Zimbabwe. Fabulous Moyo explores the broader social and political impact of prominent African Christian clergy who were sociopolitical activists such as Ndabaningi Sithole, Abel Muzorewa, and Canaan Banana. It also highlights the role of missionaries who contributed to the African struggle for independence such as Ralph Edward Dodge, Donal Lamont, and Garfield Todd. He examines the contributions of African nationalist parties and prominent politicians with Christian roots, such as Joshua Nkomo and Robert Mugabe, in the struggle for independence, and their contribution in the postcolonial era in light of their Christian heritage and the collective pre-independence nationalist ideals on nation-building and national unity.

This scholarly yet accessible book is both timely and undeniably thoughtprovoking. It irrevocably draws the reader not only to the history of Christian sociopolitical involvement in Africa but also sheds light on the seeds of the continent's current state of affairs. -
Dr Ben Shikwati, Kenyatta University, Nairobi, Kenya

Fabulous Moyo is teaching and research fellow at George Whitefield College, South Africa, and also serves as Extraordinary Senior Lecturer at North-West University, Potchefstroom, South Africa, in the Faculty of Theology.

Published 2017

Paperback ISBN: 978 0 7188 9493 1
PDF ISBN: 978 0 7188 4585 8